A Masterclass in Dramatic Writing

A Masterclass in Dramatic Writing addresses all three genres of dramatic writing—for theater, film, and TV—in a comprehensive, 14-week masterclass for the dramatic writer.

Including new material alongside revised, extended selections from Janet Neipris' original and much loved book *To Be a Playwright*, this volume takes the writer week-by-week up to a first draft and rewrite of a dramatic work.

Brand new chapters include:

- Preface: the moral responsibility of the artist
- Introduction: one writer's life
- Creating complex characters
- Comedy
- Putting it all together: the making of a play—*A Question of Country*
- Checkpoints
- Lessons from master teachers and students
- Adapting from fact, fiction, and further.

Adding these to selections on Character, Dialogue, Sixty questions, Endings, and Rewriting, Neipris has created a stunningly useful text which works across genres.

If your goal is a completed script to be proud of, you can have no more authoritative, inspiring, and careful guide than Janet Neipris.

Janet Neipris is an award-winning playwright and Professor of Dramatic Writing at NYU's Tisch School of the Arts. Her previous publications include *To Be a Playwright* (Routledge, 2006), *Natives* (2011), *Plays by Janet Neipris* (2000), and the musical *Jeremy and the Thinking Machine*, with Barbara Greenberg (2005). Her plays and letters are in the Theatre collection of Harvard University's Houghton Library.

Praise for this book

"Janet Neipris writes her books as she does her plays—from a joyous heart. Drawing on her long experience as both a playwright and a professor, she combines memoir and master class to teach us not only the craft of writing, but what it means to be a writer."

Lynn Ahrens,
stage- and screen-writer and lyricist
(*Ragtime, Once on this Island, Anastasia*)

"Neipris combines an impressive knowledge of dramatic form with her considerable experience as both an educator and writer to produce an invaluable guide for aspiring writers. Packed full of practical advice, insightful anecdote, illuminating examples, and discussion with other writers and teachers—this is no ordinary 'run of the mill' book. Neipris' book is pretty much the definitive statement on contemporary dramatic writing techniques."

Dr Tony Fisher,
Reader in Theatre and Philosophy,
Royal Central School of Speech and Drama

A Masterclass in Dramatic Writing
Theater, Film, and Television

A fully revised and extended second edition of *To Be a Playwright*

Janet Neipris

LONDON AND NEW YORK

First published 2017
by Routledge
2 Park Square, Milton Park, Abingdon, Oxon OX14 4RN

and by Routledge
711 Third Avenue, New York, NY 10017

Routledge is an imprint of the Taylor & Francis Group, an informa business

© 2017 Janet Neipris

The right of Janet Neipris to be identified as author of this work has been asserted by her in accordance with sections 77 and 78 of the Copyright, Designs and Patents Act 1988.

All rights reserved. No part of this book may be reprinted or reproduced or utilised in any form or by any electronic, mechanical, or other means, now known or hereafter invented, including photocopying and recording, or in any information storage or retrieval system, without permission in writing from the publishers.

Trademark notice: Product or corporate names may be trademarks or registered trademarks, and are used only for identification and explanation without intent to infringe.

First published as *To Be A Playwright* by Routledge, 2005

British Library Cataloguing-in-Publication Data
A catalogue record for this book is available from the British Library

Library of Congress Cataloguing-in-Publication Data
Names: Neipris, Janet.
Title: A master class in dramatic writing: theater, film, and television/Janet Neipris.
Description: Abingdon, Oxon; New York: Routledge, 2016. | Includes index.
Identifiers: LCCN 2015049545| ISBN 9781138918528 (hardback) | ISBN 9781138918542 (pbk.) | ISBN 9781315688435 (ebook)
Subjects: LCSH: Playwriting. | Drama–Technique. | Motion picture authorship. | Television authorship.
Classification: LCC PN1661 .N445 2016 | DDC 808.2/–dc23
LC record available at http://lccn.loc.gov/2015049545

ISBN: 978-1-138-91852-8 (hbk)
ISBN: 978-1-138-91854-2 (pbk)
ISBN: 978-1-315-68843-5 (ebk)

Typeset in Sabon
by Sunrise Setting Ltd, Brixham, UK

Dedicated to Harley, Andre, and Kaila

Contents

Contributors ix
Overview x
Preface: the moral responsibility of the artist xi
Acknowledgments xxiii

Introduction: one writer's life   1

Week 1 Beginnings   9

Week 2 Creating complex characters   18

Week 3 Dialogue   23

Week 4 Escalating conflicts   32

Week 5 Sixty questions to ask when writing a dramatic piece   38

Week 6 Putting it all together   49

Week 7 Endings   64

Week 8 Checkpoints   90

Week 9 Rewriting   93

Week 10 Adapting from fact, fiction, and further   107

Week 11 Comedy   118

Week 12 The habits of successful dramatic writers	131
Week 13 Lessons from master teachers and students	141
Week 14 To be a writer	158
Index	161

Contributors

Week 11 Comedy
Mark Ravenhill
Jenny Lumet
Tina Howe
David Ives
Phyllis Nagy
Polly Stenham
Ryan Craig
Judith Johnson
Steve Kaplan
Rajiv Joseph
Zack Udko
Julia Brownell

Week 13 Master teachers and students
Brandon Jacobs-Jenkin
Tina Howe
David Tolchinsky
Richard Walter
Barbara Greenberg
Mark Ravenhill
Kristoffer Diaz
Femi Euba
Sabrina Dawhan
Steve Waters
James Felder
Tony Fisher
Leah Franqui
Lauren Gunderson
Benjamin Goldthorpe
Robert B. Cohen

Overview

A Masterclass in Dramatic Writing is a one-semester 14-week course in playwriting, screenwriting, and writing for TV.

The goal is a completed script for theater, film, or TV. It is the only book of its kind covering all three genres, and is based on chairing and teaching at Tisch School of the Arts, New York University's Dramatic Writing Program and International Writing Program. The text takes the writer, week by week, to the completion of a first draft and one rewrite of a dramatic script. An introduction, "One writer's life," and the preface, "The moral responsibility of the artist," are assigned reading before starting. The semester's fourteen chapters are each accompanied by weekly exercises and progressive assignments.

With fourteen teaching chapters and essays, *A Masterclass* incorporates requested material from the original text of *To Be a Playwright* in addition to three-quarters new material.

Preface
The moral responsibility of the artist

What is the artist's responsibility to the public?
Why is a moral stance paramount in the arts?
Is the personal life of the author separate from their subject?
Can bad people make good art?
The artist's work is to reflect the face of society, to show us ourselves, and to create meaning so we can better understand our lives.

Morality is defined by the Oxford English Dictionary as:

> Pertaining to human character or behavior considered good or bad, and the distinction between right and wrong in relation to the actions, volitions, or character of responsible beings.

When writing dramatic scripts, you learn that character is action, and we are defined only by what we do, and not by what we say. A woman or man can claim they are "a good person" in the morning, but go home and murder their brother that night. We are our choices, and it's these choices that represent our characters' morality. Joan Didion, in her book of essays, *Slouching Towards Bethlehem*, marks the beginning of adulthood as the act of taking responsibility for your decisions.

So, what is the moral responsibility of the writer? Peter Handke, the Austrian author, says this responsibility is, "To have the courage to see the truth, and the even greater courage to tell the truth." The playwright and former Czech president, Vaclav Havel, wrote, "The profound crisis of human identity brought on by living a lie is the cause of a deep ethical crisis in our society." He wrote this thirty years ago, in a book of collected essays, *Living in Truth*, but it could have been written by Sophocles in 480 BC, or St Augustine, 800 years later, and on through history. The last century experienced the bloodiest wars ever and we are engaged in widespread and continued armed conflicts in this century. We have to question, for example, where the ethics are in what we have done to our environment, both through waste and the decimated landscape caused by war. This issue was effectively explored in a documentary recently viewed at the Environmental Film Festival in Washington, D.C., *Scarred Lands, Wounded Lives*. This film was produced by friends, octogenarians Alice and Lincoln Day, who have been environmentalists all their lives. They have lived by their beliefs, without a car or clothes dryer, and planting an organic garden in the middle of Washington, D.C., in what was meant as the concrete driveway for a vehicle. Their actions represent them.

A moral stance is paramount for writers. We're meant to be truth-tellers and soul-searchers. We are holding up a light to the fissures in people's lives, as Chekhov acknowledged, saying,

> We hear and feel along with you. You are not imagining this. You are not alone. The arts can and should show us our humanity. So, go out and question the universe, know what you stand for, have faith in your convictions, and be true to yourself and your inner voice.

What, then, about the personal life of the artist? The school of New Criticism, formulated from the 1940s to the 1960s, believed writing should be separated from the artist, and was meant to stand complete. In our current age of politicians gone awry, it might be a relief for them to be judged solely on the basis of their political achievements. There is, indeed, a school of thought, which believes the personal is private, and should not be considered in judging our efficacy. Many who lived through McCarthyism in the 1950s would be on the side of never mixing the personal with art. Freedom of expression is one of our major precepts. The incendiary visual-arts critic Joan Altabe asks, "Can Bad People Make Good Art?" This was in response to a cancelled display of paintings at the University of Maine when the school's president discovered the artist was a prison inmate who had killed a state trooper twenty-five years earlier. And what about the artist Degas or the poet Ezra Pound, both known for their anti-Semitism? Should this be factored into their art? Is our personal life separate from our art, and is it "nobody's business," as recently stated in the fervor of our recent political elections?

The writer's responsibility is to reflect the face of society, to show us ourselves, to create meaning so we can better understand our lives. This does not mean simply photographing reality. I tell my students reality is never an excuse for art; otherwise, people could just open up the windows and peer out. Mere documentation does not add to our insight, unless it is meant to be selective documentation. At the same time, it's not the artist's business to present a solution, but rather to posit questions and make us think. I can't abide the kind of theater and film that substitute style for story.

Currently, there is "in vogue" a kind of play whose subject is the disconnection of society, so the author writes in random and broken sentences, meaning to simulate the fracture and isolation in our lives. But we already know that. That is only a situation, and as such, is only a beginning condition. Aristotle believed good drama requires catharsis, demanding the audience suffer with the character, so as to understand what he or she is going through. It means we are alive to the problem and its danger of devastation. Not to question is the equivalent of seeing a destitute person, and shaking your head muttering, "I'm so sorry," and walking away. In a moral universe we go beyond.

J. Bronowski, scientist and philosopher, in his first book, *Science and Human Values*, takes as his theme the crisis of self-confidence that springs from each man's wish to be a person, in the face of the nagging fear that, as science shows, he is a biological machine. But, as he states in a later book, *The Identity of Man*, we are machines at birth, but become distinct individuals through experience. Our morality is formed every time we choose one action over another, or refuse to take a stand. The writer's task is to unmask, to find the subtext, to dig vertically rather than sliding across the universe horizontally. Part of our work is to find our uniqueness by scaling the heavens. This means, as artists, we are out on the open road searching for knowledge, meaning, and understanding in the face of uncertainty. To leave the scene of a crime or, to ignore it, is its own immorality. Be audacious, be dangerous, go to the edge! Apollinaire wrote at the beginning of the nineteenth century:

> Come to the edge.
> We might fall.
> Come to the edge.
> It's too high!
> Come to the edge!
> So they came and he pushed
> and they flew.

Difficult times have historically produced the most daring work, because unethical behavior angers the engaged among us, demanding our response. It is one of the reasons the Holocaust has been so represented in literature and art, as has slavery, apartheid, and war. Artists have traditionally stood up and railed against injustice. If ever there was a moment in our history for the artist, it is now. On the global stage, we are hungry, as the politicians tell us, for change. If so, then let the artists lead the way, reminding us how we came to where we are, and of a time when choice was in front of us, before we slammed the door on it. The writer posits questions about a better, or at least different, future.

Friedrich Schiller in his essays, *Letters Upon the Aesthetic Education of Man*, writes persuasively about moral dignity. We create art, he says, to capture beauty and truth, harking back to Keats's "Ode On A Grecian Urn." We make art to preserve society, rather than destroy it. In both our lives and our art, we are either on the side of the angels or not; and all the fabric of our identity is woven daily, in every brush stroke and word. Every day, we are either expanding or contracting. Choose. Choose in favor of moral dignity.

"How can the writer avoid the corruption of his time?" Schiller asks, warning us not to lower our sights to necessity and fortune. We cannot create out of ambition or a willingness to be popular in the marketplace. What is in favor one moment swiftly changes with the breeze, or the whim of the new dictator, even in a seemingly democratic society. Someone says red is black, and the crowd follows. Someone else gives meaning to the meaningless, or clothes the emperor in imaginary gold. The bully says, "Follow me," and the crowd bends into the wind, as easily as those who followed any of the maniacs of history. The critic pronounces a piece "innovative and brilliant," but you fail to find the center. If it does not appear to be right, question. Believe what you perceive. How many times have we doubted someone's dubious behavior, but waited patiently through many incidents, hopefully to be proven wrong? Listen to what you experience. Trust it. To recognize the truth is moral.

Arthur Miller sets out in his plays to find the moral dilemma. He believed you couldn't write anything decent without using the question of "right or wrong?" as the basis. From the Greeks to Eugene O'Neill and Tennessee Williams, there is a questioning. Miller goes on to say:

> All plays we call great or serious are ultimately involved with some aspect of a single problem, and it is this: How may a man make of the outside world a home? How and in what ways must he struggle, what must he strive to change and overcome within himself and outside himself if he is to find safety, love, the sense of soul, and a sense of identity and honor?

If the stage and screen are places for ideas and the intense exploration of man's fate, where is the location for entertainment in literature or the stage, what some call "the good read, the page turner," or "sheer fun"? I would speculate every author has a moral stance, even Danielle Steele. All art is generated by a point of view.

When I think of moral backbone, I reflect on those kinds of passages in drama that make us more human and less alone. We want to create moments in our work that illuminate the fissures. The largest gap is that which exists between any two individuals, and our work is to breach it.

In William Maxwell's short novel *So Long, See You Tomorrow*, there is a beginning section where a young boy is brought out of his room to meet his new stepmother, shortly after his own mother's death. The hero, in describing the moment, says how he longs to go back through the door to where it was still the time before his mother died; but that door has closed behind him. He can't go back into that room.

Raymond Carver, in his short stories, focuses on characters who, just when they think that things will be the same forever, are shaken by an event into the realization that things will never be the same again. In Thornton Wilder's *Our Town*, Emily, now dead, elects to go back and watch one day in her life, and is decimated by our lack of attention to one another. Or there's the moment in *The Glass Menagerie* when Amanda, after all her efforts, learns the gentleman suitor for Laura is not available. Hope is dashed and we're left bleeding on the ground with Amanda and Laura. These are the instances that show us our faces and the cracks in our souls.

I will never forget the moment in Neil Simon's *Plaza Suite* when the hero, played by George C. Scott in the performance I saw at Circle in the Square in New York, is at the Plaza Hotel in New York celebrating an anniversary with his wife, played by Maureen Stapleton. He is despondent and his wife says she doesn't understand. He has everything he always wanted—a fine position, a wonderful family, a beautiful home, travel—"You have it all," she tells him. "What else could you want?" she asks. Scott takes a deep breath, and then, his powerful face turns all soft, and he melts, saying in almost a whisper—this powerful giant of a man—"I just want to do it all over again." It is one of the best moments in theater, one of longing and loss, and the reason why every writer from Euripides to Chekhov to Williams to O'Neill and to Albee is searching with his own flashlight for the same such moment—the one where the everyday bleeds at the heart. Martha, near the end of Albee's play *Who's Afraid of Virginia Woolf?*, pleads with her husband to have her fantasy reinstated, the rebirth of their imaginary son. "You didn't have to kill him," she cries, and he only answers, without emotion, "*Requiescat in pace.*"

Arthur Miller says tragedy arises when we are in the company of a man who has just missed accomplishing his joy—but the joy must always be possible, within his reach. That's what makes it tragic, what breaks our hearts in the theater. Drama celebrates struggle. Sometimes, what is won is not the thing the character went after, but the other. People miscalculate. The timing is off. It comes, but it comes too late. We are always looking in front of our right shoulder, but what we want often arrives from behind the left. That is what gives us hope, the possibility that keeps us going.

We write to posit moral dilemmas. During the summer of 1987, shortly after the end of the Cultural Revolution and two years before the Tiananmen Square event, I was invited to China with a group of American writers and scholars to teach young screenwriters. During that time, I became friends with my Chinese translator; however, towards the end of our stay a curious incident occurred that was the genesis for my play *A Small Delegation.*

In a desire to help my new friend in this post-Cultural Revolution time, when goods were still scarce, I gave her a gift that was politically incorrect. It was explained I had not given the same gift to every academic official at the institute where we were teaching. Subsequently, it seriously endangered her job as a university teacher and translator, because she accepted the gift. In developing the play, I posed the question: what if a well-intentioned American goes to China meaning to do good, and in so doing, causes tragedy?

Is she to blame?

From the original incident, I constructed the play, telling the story of a small group of Americans who go to Beijing the summer before Tiananmen Square, and the developing friendship between an American professor, Remy, and her Chinese translator, Sun, and the limits of East/West exchange. Remy thinks because she can recite the history of China in one breathless monologue, that she understands the country.

"I understand this place, you know," says Remy, the American professor.

> I studied all year before we came. I read every history book about China. Everyone who ever took a ride down the Yangtze River has written a book and I've read it. Test me. Go ahead. (Continuing rapidly) The Opium War, 1839–1842, the Taiping Rebellion, 1850–1864, the Sino-Japanese War 1894–95, 1908. the Empress

Dowager dies, 1912, the child Emperor, Pu Yi, as seen in *The Last Emperor*.

But you can't locate a country's soul in history books. In the end, Remy fails to understand the differences between the two cultures and ruins her translator's life. Sun loses her university teaching job and is sent to the far off province of Gansu. Remy, the American, meant well, but nobility of intention is never enough.

The translator, Sun, questions whether morality is synonymous with truth.

> It's strange that in other countries they study the Orient, but here in the Orient we see no need to study ourselves; instead, our scholars go to Harvard and study with American Orientalists and then come home and teach us ourselves reflected. (Beat) You know, we invented gunpowder, but then the British came a thousand years later with cannons and everyone forgot we were the place where it began... How can we be a third world country if we were the first?

A current play, *A Question of Country*, takes place in South Africa during and shortly after the apartheid years. It tells of the ultimately impossible friendship between a black woman and a white woman, who together start a massive grass-roots movement. The play is based on a true story that was brought to me. Frustrated in writing within the confines of the facts, I was later given permission to change names and incidents.

In the actual script, Julia, a white woman, is a nurse at Groote Schuur Hospital in Cape Town, working on the black side of the hospital. The units were divided, *blanc* and *nieblanc*. The young white doctor addresses her.

DOCTOR

Request refused. Afrikaans, everyone. They think they can just walk in and get treated.

JULIA

True.

DOCTOR

There's need and need, and not all needs are equal. Right, nurse?

JULIA

What about the baby from Nyanga?

DOCTOR

These mothers get hysterical over a hiccough.

JULIA

I examined him this morning. He has a serious pneumonia.

DOCTOR

Well he's recovered. Sent home.

JULIA

Miraculous.

DOCTOR

Oh, miracles are our job. Say, don't worry about the black babies. They'll have another one next week. They pop them out like rabbits.

(JULIA exits into next scene)

TIME: IMMEDIATELY FOLLOWING

PLACE: TOWNSHIP, OUTSIDE CAPE TOWN.

(JULIA knocks on an imaginary door.)

TOWNSHIP WOMAN (O.S.)

(Answering from behind the door)

Who's that?

JULIA

The nurse from the hospital.

TOWNSHIP WOMAN (O.S.)

What you want, Lady?

JULIA

Open the door.

TOWNSHIP WOMAN (O.S.)

I did nothing bad. I'm a good Christian.

JULIA

I want to see how your baby is.

TOWNSHIP WOMAN (O.S.)

I'm a good woman.

JULIA

Your baby is sick.

TOWNSHIP WOMAN (O.S.)

Yes, indeed. Indela inde. You want to see my sick baby?

(TOWNSHIP WOMAN opens the door a crack)

Come, Lady, look at my sick baby.

(SHE points to a carpet rolled up by the door)

Well go ahead and look.

(SHE opens the door farther, unrolls the carpet to reveal a dead baby)

Dead on the way home, right on the bus, right in my arms, right on Voortrekker Road.

JULIA

So sorry.

TOWNSHIP WOMAN

Yes, shame [What a pity].

JULIA

Come on Mama. We're going back to the hospital.

(JULIA rolls up the carpet with the dead baby in it. The TOWNSHIP WOMAN pushes JULIA aside and finishes the rolling herself)

TOWNSHIP WOMAN

But, Lady, the baby's all dead.

JULIA

Well that's the point now, isn't it? Don't be afraid. Come on.

(The two go off carrying the rolled carpet between them, and enter into next scene immediately following)

PLACE: STEPS OF GROOTE SCHUUR HOSPITAL, CAPE TOWN

(JULIA and TOWNSHIP WOMAN with carpet approach the entrance to the hospital. DOCTOR comes down the steps to meet them)

DOCTOR

There's a problem, Mama?

JULIA (TO TOWNSHIP WOMAN)

He's asking "Ingxaki?"

DOCTOR

Can I help you?

JULIA

He is asking, "Can I help you?" "Njani?"

(TOWNSHIP WOMAN shakes her head)

DOCTOR

And your baby? Howzit?

JULIA

In here. The baby is here. Here is the baby. Here is the miracle. What a miracle. Who could believe it? (Pointing to carpet)

(JULIA starts to unroll carpet, signals to the TOWNSHIP WOMAN to help. Together they unroll the carpet, revealing the dead baby)

JULIA

And this, Doctor, is what your apartheid has done to our country. (Beat) I quit.

(Julia then chooses to go into the countryside and imposes herself on the black community, who at first think she's a spy. Also, if they are seen speaking with a white woman, they could be killed, as well as the township woman)

The same as Remy in *A Small Delegation*, Julia, out of arrogance, thinks she understands everything. But something devastating happens when she convinces the people in a township to build a school. At that time, schools weren't allowed in the townships. Good intentions again ruin someone's life.

Near the conclusion of the play, with the end of apartheid in sight, and nothing to fight against together, the friendship between Julia and Nabuntu crumbles. Nabuntu pulls away from Julia to forge new roads on her own, but Julia insists they are still like sisters in the following scene.

JULIA

I'm not political, Nabuntu. I only care about helping.

NABUNTU

Well I *am* political. That's where we differ.

JULIA

I hear they are in talks. DeKlerk hushed Mandela out of jail.

NABUNTU

They all fart words out their asses.

JULIA

Back when, I came calling through the fields, and you came running towards me, and we've been together since. Admit it. My own sister couldn't be more of a sister.

NABUNTU

True. We're Siamese twins; our hearts are attached; only our heads are separate. (Beat) It's not that you're not appreciated, Julia, but in the end, you're the wrong color... for me. You're not black, nieblanke. Some say you use your privileged liberalism only to protect your own status, like "Oh bad apartheid, let us help the poor blacks."

JULIA

That's not what I think.

NABUNTU

I have no idea what you think.

You write to question, to peel the layers until the truth explodes from the characters. What did I learn in the writing? That for all the fighting against apartheid, little changed for the blacks in their everyday lives. Race and class forever mark our days, and questions of economics and justice continue to be affected by them. For some people, that will never change. So what can the artists do in the face of such unpleasant truths? Put them before the faces of our audiences, hoping they have the courage to see it.

Adapted from speech to the Ethics Symposium,
Prindle Institute for Ethics,
DePauw University, Indiana, April 4, 2008

Acknowledgments

My thanks to the following for their support and advice:
Tina Howe, Barbara Greenberg, Victor Lodato, Craig Carnelia, Brandon Jacobs-Jenkin, Zack Udko, Jim Houghton, Elizabeth Diggs, Len Jenkin, Mark Ravenhill, Marius Von Mayenburg, Lynn Ahrens, Rajiv Joseph, Kris Diaz, Annie Baker, Richard Walter, Richard Wesley, David Grimm, Coleen Schain, Janet Rodgers, Polly Pen, Susan Blummaert, Anthony Banks, Judith Johnson, Sheryl Antonio, David Zaks, Leah Franqui, Aditya Rawal, Talia Rodgers. To the Deans at the Tisch School of the Arts—the late Dean David Oppenheim, Dean Mary Schmidt Campbell, and current Dean Allyson Green.

Special thanks also to Rita Goldberg, Friends of the Hudson Valley (FOHV), Gregory Albanis, Rick Harrison, Katheen Kayse, Hope Hughes, Jack Garrity, Tom Rosato, Bradley Jacobs, Jack Bamberger, Frank Dunn, and Hans Lupold.

This book was supported by The Global Research Institute Fellowships (GRI) at NYU, Jair Kessel, and Katy Fleming, and the NYU Global sites, Berlin and Florence. In Berlin, Dr Gabriella Etmektsoglou. In Firenze, Ellen Toscano, Stefania Bacci, and Lucia Ferrante.

My editors at Routledge, Talia Rodgers, Stacey Walker, and Kate Edwards.

Masterclass was completed with the constant cheer and encouragement of my best teachers—daughters Cynthia, Carolyn, Ellen, and Barbara, my assistant Tasha Gordon-Solmon, and all my students.

Always there is Donald, my love and warrior companion.

Janet Neipris, New York City, 2016

Introduction

One writer's life

It all began when the Mattapan Free Library opened its doors on the street next to ours. Once a week the "Library Lady" read a story, followed by "I am thinking of a number." If you guessed the number, and trusted the Lady to be telling the truth, you got to take the book home for a week. And so followed a childhood where books were free. With your library card you could take out as many as you could carry. Rapidly, I went through all the books on the lives of composers, from Bach to Verdi, followed by the "Peggy" books. Peggy was a journalist whose adventures were detailed in a series, *Peggy Covers The News, Peggy Covers Washington...* you get the idea. This was followed by the Sue Barton series, about a nurse. I skipped the Nancy Drew mystery series—in retrospect, clearly interested only in career women— moving on to the Louisa May Alcott books. Miss Alcott, a local Massachusetts author, and a woman besides, drew me in. A woman could be a writer? This was before I went to college and had even heard of Virginia Woolf. *Little Women* was my favorite, like it was many young girls of the time. I dreamed of being like Jo, the writer.

It seemed a perfectly natural activity when I went on to adapt *Little Women* as a play, producing it on the front porch of our three-decker house in Boston, paying the neighborhood kids a quarter each to attend the show. Later, while an undergraduate at Tufts University, I was "a kind of a writer" and studied with poet John Holmes, with tuition aid from Women's Scholarship Association (WSA), founded in 1907 with a mission of "furthering higher education for Boston's Jewish women 'in need'." Having "run away" to college, despite my family's pleas to be a bookkeeper like my mother, I filled the "in need" bill. Was I a true writer yet in college? By definition I was, already writing short stories, and, as president of the English Club,

2 Introduction

I introduced poet Robert Frost in Goddard Chapel on campus, where he read *The Road Not Taken* in his gravelly voice.

It was, however, the 1950s, and my ambitions lay more with the current American dream for women as homemakers. So, despite the offering of a post-grad fellowship at Tufts, and now with the desired "Mrs" degree, as well as pregnant with our first child, I took the more traveled road. The idea of becoming a writer was nowhere on my radar. That was a tale in a storybook, like Jo in *Little Women* or the Amherst, Massachusetts poet Emily Dickinson. I had already chosen a full-fledged career as wife, mother, and chief car-pool driver of a Buick Vista-Cruiser station wagon, transporting three energetic children up and down Route 128 in Boston, for a legion of lessons. But, I had this nagging feeling I was inhabiting the wrong life.

That was when luck struck. Graduating as an English major, and now a member of WSA, the group "trotted" me out at every opportunity as "The Scholarship Girl." For their many fundraisers, I would write and deliver impassioned speeches about how the opportunity had changed my life. This was true, and, as it turned out, was excellent training for what lay in the future.

With the fiftieth anniversary of the group approaching, they asked if I could write a show about women in education. *You were a writer in college, weren't you? You write all those dramatic speeches, don't you?* Could I write a show? This woman, who was the original song-and-dance kid, seeing every musical MGM ever made, then recreating the shows in our kitchen? I was Ginger Rogers and Fred Astaire dancing "cheek to cheek" and Rita Hayworth in *Cover Girl* singing "Long Ago And Far Away." My favorites were the films about Tin Pan Alley composers like Irving Berlin, going door-to-door trying to sell their songs. My parents were a willing audience. My mother, who had little romance in her life, was in love with movie musicals. My father, one terrific dancer and a shoe salesman by trade, had a magnificent voice and filled in as the cantor during High Holidays at our synagogue. His own father was a violinist, and I would later learn my great-grandfather was a musician and composer in Russia. So perhaps it was in the genes.

It was expected this show for WSA, highlighting twentieth-century women in education, would use existing music from American musicals, together with new lyrics and an original book. No one asked if I could play the piano. Well, I couldn't exactly, because I couldn't read music, but I did play by ear. Whenever visiting a friend who had a piano, I would beg to play. *Ask me to play anything. The score of* Oklahoma *or* Gilbert and Sullivan, *or name a famous opera aria.*

Just name it and I'll play it. When you play by ear, it's as though you are picking the notes straight out of the air. They just come to you.

The Schlesinger Library at Radcliffe, newly established in 1965 to document women's history, granted access to their collection. After some research, and armed with the embarrassingly sentimental title, *A Time to Remember*, I began outlining the show. The first song was to be about women demonstrating for the right to vote, but a strange thing happened. Original music began coming to me, rather than the expected notes of existing music. So I wrote the notes crudely, using the basic G-clef images, remembered from music appreciation in grammar school: EGBDF—*Every Good Boy Does Fine*. And the music just kept happening with subsequent songs. Next, a friend offered her piano, another volunteered to do the musical notation, and I was off writing a show about the rise of the Women's Rights movement and the rebellion of the housewife. Looking back, one lyric was:

> I can't decide whether to serve the potatoes instant, mashed or frozen French-fried.

A Time To Remember was presented in the main ballroom of the Statler Hilton Hotel in Boston in the spring of 1967, attended by 1,000 women, together with the good fortune that the guest of honor that day was Boston Globe theater critic Elliot Norton. After the show, beckoning to me in that assured way aristocratic Bostonians have, Mr Norton invited my future:

> You are a writer. See me in my office at Boston University on Monday at 1pm. No charge. Professional courtesy.

He took me on as a special student in playwriting, and I wrote my first play *Rousing Up the Rats Again*, based on Camus's metaphorical novel about World War II, *The Plague*. And that's how it really started. That first play eventually gained me entrance into Brandeis's MFA program in playwriting at thirty-seven years old. And Mr Norton became my good friend and advocate the rest of his living years.

How do you know you're a writer? It's not simply identifying as such at parties and on your tax forms. It's not having an idea for a dramatic piece. A student once entered my college writing workshop with four years of notebooks filled with ideas for projects. He never, however, succeeded in writing one page. How do you know you are the real thing? Certainly not by the presence of pure pleasure or finicky fame.

As Richie Walter, head of screenwriting at UCLA says, "Most writers hate writing. It's having written we like."

You know you're a writer when ideas keep insisting themselves and you write "Page 1." Or, when once you get started, you often can't pull yourself away from the piece and lose track of all time, or you think of it when you are on the train or in the shower. You keep considering how you can make it better. Then, once the first draft is written, you obsessively rewrite the first scene or the last, or the missing one, and then "cut off the fat," all the while thinking of better titles or a more apt final scene. In all the dramatic forms, you eliminate whatever does not impassion you. What is left is the real writer, and then it's your obligation to make it sing.

When was I first certain I was a real writer and not one masquerading as such? Entry into a major MFA writing program didn't do it. All it did was escalate the terror that I would soon be found out to be a fraud, a moderately talented mistake. Even then I knew that a "moderate and competent talent" was not good enough in this field. The one thing a writing program did do, however, was require writing. In real life nothing is required. You're on your own.

Was it after Brandeis's theater department chose to produce two of my plays? That was a start, but there was still the distressing fear the whole affair was a "one or two nighter," and the Emperor would soon be found to be *sans* clothes. The surety of you as a writer only comes with repeated evidence. It's much like believing we are loved. If we indeed are, or deserve to be, we have to see it demonstrated over and over again to own it.

It wasn't until my first plays were going into production in Chicago at the Goodman Theatre in 1975, owing to the generosity of my professor, Israel Horovitz, who recommended the work and at the same time got me a first agent, Mary Dolan at the Gloria Safier Agency. I remember that airplane trip from New York, scared, and wishing I could return to my previous life where I was baking apple pies. But I couldn't go back through that door. It had closed behind me, and I had become a playwright.

This was reinforced, shortly after, in 1976, by the establishment of a legendary writing workshop at Goddard College in Vermont, the nation's first low-residency MFA in creative writing. The program was the brainchild of poet Ellen Bryant Voigt. Students would come together in Vermont with faculty twice a year, summer and winter, and, in between, correspond with the assigned faculty, sending pages, receiving critiques, rewriting and moving forward on their manuscripts. During residency there were readings, lectures, conferences, visiting professionals, and the usual mischief prevalent in writing colonies. Ellen, as it turned out, was a genius at identifying writers who were on their way up. What a community it was! For fiction writing there were John Irving, Richard Ford, and the Wolf Brothers, Greg and Tobias. Non-fiction was the province of Richard Rhodes from Kansas, who had already gathered praise for his book about the Donner Party, *The Ungodly*, and who would go on to write twenty-five more books and win a Pulitzer Prize. Donald Hall, Philip Levine, Louise Gluck, Barbara Greenberg, and Robert Haas taught the poets. It was Barbara, a close and valued friend, who recommended they have someone for playwriting, and that's what brought me to the hills of Vermont, together with a golden group of serious and ambitious writers. They were to become the forefront of America's literary scene. We shared a common distinction. We were all considered "promising." Our days and nights were about words—our students and ours. It turns out the company we keep often keeps us on our toes, preserving our honesty. We all had stories to tell. Dick Rhodes became a lifelong friend and mentor and Barbara already was. Without noticing, gradually your group of friends and associates grows to include many of the professionals in your field, and you are one of them.

In the end, what define you as a writer are your actions, the same as the characters in your scripts. It is a primary rule of characterization. We are what we do, not what we say. What makes up the real fabric of your days? Joan Didion wrote in *The Year of Magical Thinking*: you "have to choose the places you don't walk away from."

Look at the *Notebooks of Athol Fugard, 1960–1977*. They were the beginnings of *Blood Knot*, *Hello and Goodbye*, and *Boesman and Lena*. Read about the essence of Fugard's days, his ideas, his dreams and reflections on current history, overheard conversations, outlines for current plays, and thoughts on future ones. He is asking all the major questions of a serious writer. At the start of *Notebooks* is the following passage:

> London: Notes for a play 1960
>
> Korsten in Port Elizabeth: up the road past the big motor assembly and rubber factories, turn right down a dirt road, pot-holed, full of stones. Donkey wandering loose. Chinese and Indian grocery shops. Down this road you come to the lake – the dumping ground for waste products from the factories – a terrible smell. On the far side – like a scab on the hill rising from the water is Korsten: a collection of shanties and mud huts. No streets, no numbers. A world where anything goes – any race, any creed. When the wind blows in the wrong

> direction, the inhabitants of Korsten live with the stink of the lake.
>
> In one of these shacks at Berry's Corner are the two brothers Morris and Zachariah.

These notes were the beginnings of his play.

In the early 70s, screenwriter Paddy Chayefsky was mad at himself and American TV viewers. He was seeing the venomous spirit of Watergate and the Vietnam War infiltrate every program the broadcast networks offered, from their news shows to their sitcoms, and concluded in a typewritten note to himself that the American people didn't want "jolly, happy family type shows, but were angry and needed shows about outrage." It was then he wrote the "I'm mad as hell" speech, which would be the cornerstone of his script for the film *Network*.

The following are the initial notes I made for a TV pilot, *Hog Alley*, with my husband, Donald Wille. It was optioned by ABC TV and based on Don's experiences as an engineer in backwater Texas town.

> A hotshot MBA type from the East gets his real education when he's sent to build a dam in the middle of Texas. Picture a small town near Fort Worth, population 5,000, a Texas Timbuktu, and a construction site mired in mud, dust, and overflowing paper. On the site is a row of office trailers connected by a long passageway. Because the place looks like a pigsty, the workers have nicknamed the site "Hog Alley."

Molly Veh, a senior at Tisch School of the Arts, and finalist in their Fusion Film Festival, had the following notes for her screenplay *Bear Crossing*, which won a prize:

> Thanksgiving, and Quinn, a twenty-something bisexual woman, brings her girlfriend Teddy home to her small, conservative, Stepford-like hometown. Over the course of the weekend, the girls must confront awkward conversations, aggressive religious zealots, past friends and lovers, as well as their own insecurities with each other.

Molly writes:

> This piece was an attempt to shove myself out of my comfort zone, try my hand at writing comedy, which I'd never done before. The set up was based on a series of events in my own life, namely acquiring a girlfriend and realizing my mother would have to meet

her someday, and dozens of questions followed. What would happen if I brought a girl home to meet my extended, loud, Catholic family? Would I be able to blend my current life with my past and the people who knew me then? In the screenplay, I'll ask these questions in the most extreme and absurd way possible. How far can I push my characters, utilizing the realities of my life, before I save them from the brink of melodrama and pull them back into the hilarious realm of real life?

Where are *your* writer's notebooks? What do they say about past projects or future ones? If you already keep notebooks, save the pile of them forever. You never know when one of your stories will fly and someone will interview you and ask when you first started thinking about this idea. Often, it turns out, we were mulling over related themes since we began writing. When I look back I find the repetition of the following themes:

> *Rousing Up the Rats Again*—How can we avoid repeating history?
>
> *A Small Delegation*—Is a gift a gift if someone cannot afford to receive it?
>
> *Out of Order, After Marseilles*—How to make order of disorder.
>
> *The Agreement, Statues, Exhibition*—Where does love live?
>
> *A Question of Country, The Bridge at Belharbour*—What can we do in the face of evil?

Looking back through years of journals, I found these notes:

> 1988
>
> *It's the year before Tiananmen Square and a small American delegation comes to China to teach without totally understanding the culture, and ends up inadvertently harming one of their Chinese translators.*
>
> Became *A Small Delegation*.
>
> 1990—overheard in a department store
>
> Last week we lost everything. My husband lost his glasses and I lost my wedding band. Last week, also, everyone was nasty to me... my mother, my husband, my sister, my dear friend.

Became *The Southernmost Tip*, about a character who doesn't take responsibility for her own life. Always the victim.

1991—London, the housekeeper Elba from Portugal

My husband, he is depressed and alcoholic. I come home from work, he is drunk. I say forget supper and go to bed. I pray and pray to God to make him tired.

Used in *Look Ma We're Dancing*.

1993—character says, "The only thing that's the end of the world is the end of the world."

Used in *Almost In Vegas*, spoken by Alma.

2000—ecological disaster or perhaps a terrorist plot and much of the world is destroyed. One of the few cities remaining is Marseilles. Everything drops to there, because it's the bottom of Europe. People are displaced from their homes. New rules have to be set. Are we destined to keep repeating history?

Became *After Marseilles*, first done at the O'Neill Playwrights Conference, summer, 2002.

2005—Maya Angelou, "In order to forge a future the nation would have to honestly confront its past."

Became *A Question of Country*, about South Africa, the apartheid and post-apartheid years, and the Truth and Reconciliation Commission.

How do we know we're a writer? We know we're real because we insist on going on, despite the inevitable frustrations and heartbreaks. With regularity we swear we will never write another play, never outline another screenplay, never contemplate pitching a new idea for a TV pilot. And yet, before we know it, there we are, back in business, riding the horse again. We can't help ourselves. We wish we could, but there's a story we want to tell, and tell it we must. That's our life.
Lecture delivered at Tisch School of the Arts, Dramatic Writing Department, March 2015

Week 1
Beginnings

Finding your story and telling it

The most compelling stories are those where the characters struggle to take control of their lives. The strongest stories originate from passion. What makes you angriest? Betrayal? Mendacity? Blind ambition? Entitlement? When contemplating a new play, screenplay, or TV pilot, I often make a list of my major grievances and irritants, both personal and political, mindful that the personal *is* the political. Next, I think about life experiences that powerfully recall those same emotions. The same guidelines apply to writing spec pilots for television. *Hog Alley* was a pilot I sold to ABC, prompted by unconscionable work conditions at an engineering site in Texas where my husband was stationed. An overweight employee with a history of heart disease was made to park almost a mile away every day and walk in the summer heat on gravel paths, while the managers and top corporate people were assigned a parking space adjoining the main gate. One day the employee collapsed and died. Appalling. An event based on this story was only one incident in the pilot, but was brought to light, the same as management in the films *Silkwood* and *Network*. "How could they?" We write dramas to ask questions. Often, we are asking why someone behaves like they do.

Sometimes stories originate with dissatisfaction and a questioning of a personal or observed journey, one that began with good intentions and went sour. Was there a way the downward trajectory could have been prevented? If so, start with a character's noble intentions, but have a different result. The plot is then shaped by the actions the character takes that influence the new outcome. In that case there is the satisfaction of taking charge of the past and reordering it. That's what motivates many writers. Writing is the best revenge.

Locating the story you want to tell requires what I term "open heart surgery." You are open to your inner stirrings, indicating you are totally engaged, and will fight to the end to write this story. It is easy to detect the writer who is distanced from the fervor or ache of their subject. The lack of passion and connection to a piece evidences itself early on. When the author describes the project, the enthusiasm is absent. Then, the characters fail to take on flesh, blood, or emotion. The focus is fuzzy. The story limps along. This is often the case when I suspect a student is merely interested in their subject, but not "on fire." Eventually they will come forward, saying they want to scrap the project, because they have something they are more ardent about writing.

There are also those stories that emerge from newspapers. Take any day of the *Guardian* or *New York Times*, circle one potential story on every page, and then choose one that grabs your fancy and make an outline. I often use this as an exercise in class, and, to my surprise, some students choose to write one of those stories that resonate with them. Some of us need a little "jiggling." The news stories are the seeds, but when they fall on fertile ground, the writer is off to a beginning.

Then there are the plays, screenplays, and TV dramas and series that originate with character. It starts with us observing someone. Chekhov was the master of observation, even in his short stories, which demand compression and a swift portrayal. They are similar to the requirements of the ten-minute play. In his short story "The Lady With the Pet Dog," Chekhov begins:

> A new person, it was said, had appeared on the esplanade, a lady with a pet dog... a fair-haired young woman of medium height, wearing a beret; a white Pomeranian was trotting behind her. She walked alone.

When formulating a character, what kinds of behavior attract our attention, arousing our curiosity? Why is she acting like this? How did she become this kind of a person? How could his present actions contribute to his downfall? How will the person driven with ambition finally get stopped in their tracks? How can their own actions contribute to their disaster? How might they get into trouble and then make a correction? Will it be too late? Will they just miss their joy like one misses a train? What does our character want badly? How hard will they fight to get it? We write by asking questions. The audience is pulled inside our stories, wanting to know one thing—what happens.

Who is our protagonist? The protagonist has the most to lose. What is in danger as the main character searches for the object of their desire? What may be the barriers to success? I use the metaphor of a castle on the hill where a treasure is buried. This treasure represents the character's deepest wants. But, in order to get up that hill and into the castle, the character must slay the dragons standing in the way. Only, once they slay the first dragon, another appears in its place, and then finally a third to be conquered. These are your escalating conflicts, a requirement of drama.

I love the journey in the film *The African Queen*, adapted from C.S. Forester's novel, where this concept is clear. During World War I, two disparate characters are thrown together on a river boat in East Africa, trying to travel down the treacherous Ulana River in search of an opening to Lake Victoria, with a plan to attack a German ship. First they are confronted by one of the character's drinking problem, then mosquitoes, then leeches, then violent rapids, then Germans shooting at them, then a drought, then incessant rains and a flood. The troubles never stop. The obstacles multiply. Continuing the castle metaphor, every time we think we're safe, we're not. Or, there is the possibility that we reach the treasure and it turns out not to be what we expected, or it may not be there at all. In the case of *The African Queen*, the main characters, after overcoming a multitude of tribulations, finally reach the opening of the river onto the lake, and there is *The Louisa*, the German ship they've been trying to reach.

Only, there is one more twist. They aren't free yet. More trouble lies ahead in a spectacular and triumphant ending. The shared challenges of the journey ultimately transform the characters.

Adaptation of a novel or short story is another source (Chapter 10). If a story is not in the public domain, be prepared to deal with obtaining the rights from the author and publisher. Once you succeed in procuring the rights, there are the decisions about what to leave in, what to extract, what to completely abandon, and what to imagine.

Some scripts evolve from overheard conversations or from a single image. In those cases, the storyteller has to think backwards. Why did the conversation stick with you? What issue did it raise? If this is what you want to write about, who will populate the drama? How could these characters be tested? What will be their tragic flaw? The real question—once you have characters and conflict identified, and write the first scene—is does the script idea still excite you? Do you still yearn to write this story? Desire is always the engine.

Basing a play on a historical event requires laborious research. Count on it taking six months to a year, at a minimum. There are the obvious books and periodicals, but you can't know a country or event just by reading a book. That only gives you the facts. If it is a contemporary event, there are the possible interviews. Once those are completed, you have to select the information that may be helpful either historically, shaping characters, or establishing possible conflicts. Then there is the dilemma of how closely you have to stay with the facts (Chapter 6, "Putting It All Together"; Chapter 10, "Adaptation"). If you don't, anticipate criticism and be willing to go with the project anyways, as Oliver Stone did with his film *JFK*. Peter Morgan's drama *Frost/Nixon* is another example of selected facts. Aaron Sorkin's *Social Network* caught flak for fictionalizing events based on a true story. In the case of *The Social Network*, fiction notwithstanding, the film won the Academy Award for Best Adapted Screenplay. So take a chance, accept the consequences, and be willing to fight for your project.

If you choose to stay only with the facts, there is also a price. The true story may not be dramatically sustainable. Do you have the right to change the facts for the sake of theatricality? No one is going to sue you if you are writing about an incident in the Civil War and imagining some of it. Certainly Shakespeare did this in his history plays. However, if you claim it is a documentary, be prepared to be challenged. Note how often the term "based on" is used in plays and screenplays. This term covers a multitude of fictions. There is also the less formal TV piece, which simply states "inspired by" to provide much literary latitude.

Once you've chosen your subject, how to begin? You can't start writing the first scene until you've populated the landscape. The first questions are *who* and *where*? First, consider your protagonist. It's generally a single character, although there are examples of the buddy movie, like *Thelma and Louise*. The protagonist should be determined by their goal, and their opportunity to achieve it. Arthur Miller, in his essay "Tragedy and the Common Man," says the possibility of victory must always be there. The audience must always have empathy for the main character. This doesn't necessitate that they "like" the character, more that they understand the character's motivation. Always, I construct a backstory for characters, in order to grasp the source of their actions or longings, but also to give the text depth and specificity.

Then there's the question of how many characters you need to tell your story; and, at the same time, consider the practicality for production. One time I was writing an epic play, covering thirty years. It began with ten characters, until I was warned of the dangers inherent in writing such a large cast. Most theaters do not want or cannot sustain that production cost. So, I fused some of the characters and, at the same time, double cast them. This reduced the cast to five. When I gave the first draft to Zelda Fichandler, founder of the Arena Stage

Theater in Washington, D.C., she questioned my small cast. She suggested a play with this scope needed a cast size to fill the world I'd created. So, taking that advice, I went back to a cast of ten. It was not easily produced, but at least I was true to my original vision. In dramatic writing you're often confronted with the choice of the personal versus the commercial. Tony Kushner wasn't writing for any kind of commercial theater when he wrote *Angels in America*. My advice is never write to the fashion, but only to your own power. Fashion is fickle, particularly in film and TV. Plays, because they are the sole property of the author, encourage more originality. Historically, those writers whose work originated from their own appetites are the most successful. The only reason to write, says author Stephen Sondheim, is *love*.

Another decision regards style. What style is going to enhance your story? You have a double responsibility to both your audience and yourself not to be boring—to entertain, inform, question, illuminate, and invigorate. Remember you need to keep the audience awake. Some of the choices are naturalism, satire, the absurd, melodrama, or humor. Take, for example, the opening of Ionesco's *The Bald Soprano*, when Mrs Smith speaks.

> Good grief, it's nine o'clock. We've eaten our soup, fish, buttered potato jackets and British salad. The children have drunk British water. We stuffed ourselves this evening. All because we live in the outskirts of London and our name is Smith.

The style is clearly set here. We are in the illogical world of existential despair.

Humor can often prompt the way to tell a story the writer is avoiding, whether about war, family, or everything in between. Once, I wanted to write a play about divorce, but whenever I thought of a way into the project, it fell flat. Understanding that humor often covers deep hurts too painful to confront directly, I saw a way in. During divorce proceedings, the lawyers can become so self-enchanted and empowered by their well-prepared cases and the actual battle, the clients and their needs can be left behind. Once the legal machinery is set in motion and rapidly running, there is no room for the personal, least of all for a change of mind. The following is from my play *The Agreement*, when the lawyers, Alice and Lester, hand Sybil and Sigmund their divorce document to sign, with "It's over."

SYBIL

Wait a minute! We forgot the children!

LESTER

The children.

ALICE

The children.

SIGMUND

How could you forget the children?

ALICE

Well they're *your* children.

LESTER

You could have reminded us.

ALICE

(Holding our her list)

Look at all these items we're juggling. You need the memory of an elephant.

(Reading) She got the swings on the outdoor equipment clause.

LESTER

So he gets the children, no strings attached ...

SYBIL

I'm not giving up any children.

LESTER

We all have to make do with partial rewards.

SYBIL

Tell it to Santa Claus.

SIGMUND

The children are hers.

                    ALICE

I move we put the children on a rider.

                    LESTER

(Writing) *Ride* the children

                    SIGMUND

And it's over.

                    SYBIL

Over.

Then a few lines later, the two now alone ...

                    SYBIL

Sometimes when I'm on a date I call the man Sigmund by mistake. I forget. Maybe I'll always forget, or never forget... could you give me a lift to the airport?

                    SIGMUND

Maybe you never will. When I go to bed at night I always make sure the pillows are together, even though no one's there. Come on, Sybil... to the airport.

So, you can make the turn gently, from comedy to a sense of loss, and realize your intentions. I love this play about divorce, the way it is entertaining for the audience, was great fun to write, and, by the end, accomplishes the truth of the cracks in our lives.

Before you establish style and tone, try writing your first scene in a number of styles, determining which one works best and noting which one comes easiest to you. Ease is often an indicator of talent, because its source is instinct. Just stay with your passion and confusion and you'll find they will sort themselves out through several rewrites

I'm often asked if I make an outline for a play. Not at first. I wait until I am about three or four scenes into the play and have some kind of idea of the texture and where I might be going. An outline in a play is never a blueprint. It's simply a peg to hang your story on. Many times, I may not keep to it, because the characters often have their own minds, if fleshed out properly. But I like to have something up on the wall in front of me, even something I may change. It's a kind of a lifeline to hold onto. With screenplays, I always outline, because screenwriting is more plot-oriented. The story moves, not through dialogue, but through images. With TV, it's been my experience, other than when writing an original pilot, that you are given the storyline and characterizations and you must operate within the world of the show. Once, I was hired to write for daytime drama and handed the storyline for the next week. Being new, I was intent on showing off my talent for character, humor, and dialogue, and wrote away. I was fired two weeks later, informed I had taken too much creative license with the script. I then decided daytime drama was not for me. But it could be right for you.

Good stories work for a hundred and one reasons; but when stories fail, they often fail in similar ways. Sometimes, we start the story too early and the real story doesn't begin until we are a quarter of the way through the script. E.L. Doctorow recommends starting a story "as late as possible." By that he means nearest to the crucial action. One of my graduate students describes it as the first wheel falling off the wagon. Starting with only three wheels on your wagon, the first dramatic question is raised early on—how are you going to get where you want to go with this compromised wagon?

My former professor, playwright Israel Horovitz, taught that the dramatic question has to be established in the first ten minutes of the play. One of the characters must come forward and say something like, "I am going to bake the biggest bagel in New York and just you watch." Or, two characters in a room discuss a character that is set to enter. The one says to the other, "When Steve comes in, lets rob him, then tie him up. We may have to murder him, but lets see how things go." Next, there's a knock at the door and it's, "Hi Steve! How are you doing? Come in!" Now the audience is complicit in the secret with the characters onstage. The tension and dramatic question is clear. Will they murder Steve? An audience always stays in the theater for one reason—to see what happens.

The beginning is the most anxious and exciting time, heavy with possibility. As in the closing lines of Milton's *Paradise Lost*, when Adam and Eve enter Paradise:

> The World was all before them, where to choose
>
> Their place of rest, and Providence their guide:
>
> They hand in hand, with wandring steps and slow,
>
> Through Eden took their solitarie way.

This is the writer, embarking on the journey of creating a dramatic piece. The first draft isn't the end product of an idea. The idea will be the end product of your first draft. It's always about the process.

So, pull on your warrior boots, sharpen your pencils, and you're packed and ready to go. You are armed with one reminder: No matter what, write out of love—love for your characters, the gratification of getting a moment just right, the excitement of telling the story and the surprise of seeing where it goes, the realization of what your story is truly about, nailing the closing scene, the joy of accomplishing a first draft and writing "The End," followed by the rewrites that will sail your project home, ready for production and a life.

Lecture delivered at Beijing Film Academy, October 2014

Exercises

Identify three things that make you angriest. Next, choose the one you feel strongest about. It's helpful to recall a real situation where you observed or experienced what you'll be writing about. Now, decide on the story you might tell. Remember that the real story is only the starting point. The writer's task is to invent a dramatic story. Do not stay hostage to all the facts of the true story.

Take three pages from a newspaper. Identify one story of interest to you on each page. Next, choose one to base your story on, whether plot or character. Adapt freely from the true story. What situation has the most dramatic possibilities?

Assignment

Choose the story you want to write and complete a one-page synopsis. The synopsis should say what the story is about as well as the simple plot.

On a second page, list the major characters with descriptions. If you are creating an original TV pilot, choose a situation that promises ongoing conflict. After writing the initial one-hour pilot episode, suggest five additional episodes. In TV, producers are looking for the long-distance runners as well as possible spin-offs.

Now make a writing schedule for this week and every week thereafter. If possible, write six days a week. Set aside a minimum of three hours a day. When you are "on fire" with your project, the writing hours may very well extend.

Week 2
Creating complex characters

Questions to ask when formulating a character
Developing a complete backstory
Character as motivation, which leads to action
Identifying your hero/heroine and your antagonist

For a long time, I suggested my students begin their characterizations with a complete biography. In practice, however, after writing a number of scripts, I concluded there was a better starting point. In a play or a screenplay, the writer needs to know the story they are telling first, and then listen to that character in the first few scenes of the story. The same is true for TV pilots. However, if you are signed on for an already existing TV series, you will be given the "Bible," which contains the concept, location, bios of the characters, full episodes, synopses of potential episodes, and possibly even a pilot episode. Once the TV series is launched, the Bible is used to keep track of details about the setting. Then it is your job to stay within the boundaries of character and avoid originality. Keep originality for the dialogue. My first television assignment was with *General Hospital*. Because I was at the beginning of my career and anxious to "show my stuff," I was fired after my first assignment for "coloring outside the lines." It never made it from the page to the screen.

How do you begin developing a character? After you meet the character, open their mouths, and hear their voices. You are still in the "dating" period. This lasts through the first three or four scenes. A character needs time to evolve as you are exploring their actions on the page. These actions are the starting points that define your character.

After that, stop and answer some basic questions:

1 How would you cast the character from people in your life, on the street, on the bus or subway, from a photo, or from actors on TV, screen, and stage? If you are in auditions for a project, for example, ask the actors who come in if they have a picture/resumé you can have. This turns out to be helpful whether you are involved in casting another show or if you are just using it in forming your character physically. Get a picture of someone you feel is ideal for

Creating complex characters

the role. It's one of the first questions a director asks the writer. Get a photo from auditions, newspapers, or magazines and pin it up on your bulletin board, so your character takes on real flesh and blood, and you can visualize them going through each scene.

2   What does the character want more than anything? Why?
3   What do they wish were different about their life?
4   What dream has eluded this character so far?
5   What is one of the character's worst fears, or some of them?
6   What brings this character the most joy? Do they know this or do they discover this in the course of the story? Name the last time this character had fun.
7   What is the biggest lie they ever told? Why?
8   What makes this character the angriest? Why?
9   What is this character's strength?
10 Greatest weakness?
11 What is most appealing about this character?
12 Where were they born?
13 What has been their greatest adventure so far?
14 How does this character delude herself/himself?
15 How did this character spend the previous Christmas?
16 What secrets does this character have?
17 What are the character's plans for the future?
18 Who is envious of them in the story? Who is suspicious?
19 Ask the character to write an honest letter to their best friend, telling them the recent events in their life and how they feel about it.
20 What is their greatest ambition (which may be different than "want")?

Armed with these answers for each character, go back to the beginning and do whatever rewrites are necessary, based on your new insights. When a new character enters in one of the following scenes, allow them the same developing space.

When I am at the halfway point in a play, for example, or after Act 1, I proceed to the following biographical questions, further developing the character, requiring them to answer in the first person:

1   Tell me about your childhood. Six strong memories?
2   Describe yourself as if you were casting a character or signing in on a dating site.
3   Tell me where you were before you stepped into this story.
4   What do you read—everything from literature to "trash"?

Since you are the creator, you can now identify additional characteristics by asking the following. Make certain the voices for your characters differ. If you keep a notebook and write down conversations you overhear and the specific cadences of the people speaking, you'll begin to understand originality in voice.

1. What's at stake in the story? How far will this character go to get it?
2. Are they likely to take chances? If not, what will force or convince them to do so?
3. Describe two or three trips the character has taken and how he felt. Maybe they will read back from their diary, after you've invented the diary entry.
4. How is the character most likely to fail?
5. Do they have strength, but don't realize it yet? How will you test them in the story, allowing their strong points to evidence themselves?
6. What chances have they lost out on and why? Their dreams?
7. How do they earn their way? Do they dream of doing something else? What?
8. What are their demons? Why? They usually come from past experiences. Which ones contributed to the demons?
9. What do you admire about the character?
10. George Balanchine said "Only God creates; the artist reveals." What is your character's secret?

As you're formulating your characters, do so with compassion. We all are heroic in the battles we wage as humans.

A writer must know their character intimately—how they would act in given situations and how they came to be this way. So complete each character's backstory that not only explains their demons, but their desires as well. Where are the holes that need filling in this person? The questions continue as you go about breathing life into your characters. The past is alive in the present.

What makes a character complex? Knowing their interior life. Characters consist of wants, fears, strengths, and weaknesses. If you can figure out where these are in your first draft, you are halfway there. Complexity is achieved by realizing there are warring elements in each character. For example, a character can be very ambitious and at the same time ethical. If other characters in the story are reaching their goals through unscrupulous means, what will your character choose in order to remain competitive? What may be the consequences of the two choices the character is facing? Or, a single parent has a

Creating complex characters

child with dyslexia, but not badly enough that the state will approve funding for a private school and/or extra help. The mother is an excellent parent and provider. Should the mother leave her work as a gym teacher to home-tutor him, and thereby put them below the poverty line? Or should she take on a second job to pay for the tutoring, but then be away from home every night? Or should she try to find the child's father, who abandoned them earlier; but what might that result in? How she chooses reflects her character. Or, a woman who has been unhappy in her life for a long time finally decides, in order to save herself, she must divorce her husband. But wait! He is then diagnosed with cancer. Will she stay or leave? Our job as dramatists is to give good people tough choices, and those choices define us.

In developing a character, what you want is emotional authenticity. In writing the script you are schizophrenic in that you are taking on the voice and personality of that character in every speech and action and experiencing every feeling. In the same way Meryl Streep always inhabits her characters, you must occupy yours physically and emotionally. That means you are in a perpetual birth cycle or *playing* all the *parts* in your script when each speaks.

There are three ways to show the complexities of your character:

1 What the character does.
2 What the character says about themselves, always looking for the subtext.
3 What others say about the character. Then we are expected to discern if these others are telling the truth or not. If not, what would be their motivation for lying? You, as the as the architect of these characters, supposedly know them inside and out.

Early on, decide who is the protagonist and who is the antagonist. Remember that the protagonist has the strongest want and the most to lose. There are no passive main characters. The antagonist, the one who gets in the way of your hero, must have characteristics that will oppose the motivations of the protagonist. Keeping this in mind early allows you to fashion characters that will have traits that are in opposition to each other. Then try and figure out how they came to be who they are. A good exercise is to make a list of character traits that are in opposition to each other and use this for every project.

What makes a character compelling? The most interesting people are those who take control of their own lives. Is there a moment in your story when this happens for one of the characters and why? What forces this action? We want our audiences to understand our characters, but not necessarily like them at all times. Are you always likable? No, because you are human and sometimes flailing in the face of the scheme of things. We are not only complex, we are unsure where certain choices may land us. A character can only speculate. It is this uncertainty that makes for drama. There are often a dozen ways things can turn out. You, as the author can make things happen the way you want. How many people can do that?

After your characterizations are complete, your next task is to devise a plot that challenges your characters. We are all tested in the mountains we're forced to climb in adversity. Happiness goes in a straight line and is ultimately boring dramatically. What is your character really made of? Iron or clay? We are all something at the very bottom. Think of some of your friends. How are they likely to act if the going gets rough? What is their true mettle?

The author's best tool is observation. We want to know why someone is acting the way they are. We are always looking for the clues, the whys. Real life is the best laboratory. Literary and personal experience is at the root of all character development. Why makes a person betray another? It is not only about what they want, but why they are willing to risk losing a friendship by betrayal. They must think the prize is worth the loss. But why?

It's crucial that a writer reads. Writing is an intellectual as well as an artistic endeavor. How better to think about characterization than by studying the characters depicted by the pantheon of Greek dramatists like Aeschylus and Euripides, the great classical writers like Dickens and Tolstoy, contemporary novelists and short-story writers like Raymond Carver, Junot Diaz, and Toni Morrison. You cannot depend solely on personal observation, but can take advantage of the great character writers of the past. Your bedside and all the flat surfaces in your living space should be overtaken by piles of books—those you have read and those you plan on reading.

Exercises

Answer all the questions asked about character in this chapter. Then create a biography for each character.

Assignment

Write the second five pages.
   Read the first ten pages aloud for a critique.[*]

---

[*] Critique can be in class, in a writer's group, or one on one with a colleague.

Week 3
Dialogue

How characters conceal and reveal—text and subtext
What we say and why we say it
Finding the music of individual voices
How real should dialogue be?
What to avoid when writing dialogue

Characters speak in order to relay information both factual and emotional. Dialogue can also be used to deceptively give information in order to gather support, purposely mislead, or gain intimacy.

Keep in mind the above purposes for dialogue. Each has its own subcategory of motivation. What do I mean? For example, if a character wants to get someone to agree with him, he might give fabricated information or exaggerate in order to garner sympathy. Candidates running for office may give information that is only a half-truth. Read the newspapers daily to see direct quotes from politically positioned characters. For a good exercise, try to figure out what could be the possible truths in the subtext. The truth is often the hardest thing to find in any character's dialogue. Just because a character says something, we cannot presume it is the truth. In fact, it is often quite the opposite. David Mamet says characters most often speak in order to conceal.

For example, there is the character who has been previously remote. What could the motivation be in suddenly wanting intimacy? It could result from the character truly feeling abandoned and alone. On the other hand, the intimacy may be false, with the desired effect of a closeness meant to gather confidential information, or to win sexual favor, or to borrow money. The writer is the one who must know what is going on inside his character's head, and exactly what the character wants and why. Once you know the character's motivation, you choose the route for them to get what they want, with either dialogue or action. This choice by your character then comes to define them. What we choose is who we are.

In what instances might a character reveal the absolute truth? When do you? Notice the next time you are honest and determine your motivation. What is it you want? Pity? Respect? Love? Intimacy? Forgiveness? Or maybe it's to get a raise or to get invited to the party.

Only the author knows whether his/her characters are telling the truth, and sometimes, not initially. The truth may be uncovered later in the script. Either the author knows it at the start or discovers it in the writing of the piece. What are some of the reasons characters skirt the truth? Exaggeration may inflate their ego and/or standing. Sometimes it's an effort to hide their emotional state, not wanting to make themselves vulnerable. For example, a woman is an alcoholic and has "disappeared" for two months. In actuality she is at a rehab facility, but doesn't want her friends and workplace to know. Think of the stories she may invent in order to hide the truth and the possible consequences. Or in some instances, the character may minimize an occurrence or slightly alter the facts, in order to exonerate them. An untrue story, as in malicious gossip, having unscrupulous facts bandied about, may undermine another character because of either revenge or wanting to maneuver ahead of that character. Think of all the reasons you might want to undermine someone. How could you achieve that? Count the awful ways.

Good dialogue writing is a matter of characters speaking in an original way, true to their own voice. Clichéd dialogue comes from "easy writing," somewhat akin to elevator music or "easy listening." It often originates from a lack of "selection." The author chooses the dialogue that comes out of their character's mouth effortlessly. It's the first thing the writer thinks of, but has no relation to the character's individual voice. A good test is to give the line to one or two other characters in the script. If it's interchangeable, it lacks originality. When I come across flat or clichéd dialogue in a student's work, I write, "translate." This means "please rewrite in more original language." Can you tell who is speaking by their cadence, tone, and language?

Basically, every line of dialogue should either illuminate character or move the plot. Reality is never an excuse for art. Just because a character may say something in reality does not give the dialogue a raison d'etre.

Selection plays a major part in dialogue. Recently, an acquaintance gave me a copy of their new, self-published book. It was such a thicket of words, you needed a rake to go through every paragraph. Self-publishing is fine, but make certain you have an editor checking you. The first rule of dialogue is "do not overwrite." Throw away your darlings. Be disciplined. You are just telling a story, not writing a thesis.

"Talking heads" can occur in all dramatic forms. It happens when imagery is lost due to long sections of dialogue, and the audience is left with just two heads communicating. The writer's task, again, is to select that dialogue which advances character or plot. Ordinary conversation does not belong in a dramatic piece. It is, however, sometimes used in daytime TV drama. In this case, the viewer may make more frequent exits and re-entries, multitasking, and has to be frequently reminded of what has just happened on the TV screen and who is speaking. Make your own work lean and mean. Excessive "talk" will only make your script dense, pulling away from the focus and the forward movement. The weight of every word counts. SELECT. You cannot throw out there every word your character could possibly utter and then ask your audience to sift through and edit your work in order to make sense of it. Otherwise, we could just open our windows and listen in on what people are saying.

Individuation of voices demands that the dialogue is coming from inside the character and not from your computer keys. This is what makes dialogue sing. The dramatic writer always hears the character's voice. Keep a journal where you record the exact rhythms of different people's dialogue. Remember some of these so you can use them in your writing, making certain each character in your piece speaks differently and has an individual cadence.

In addition, in your editing and rewriting process, make sure you are not saying the same thing in three different ways. An example of this kind of dialogue would be:

> You bring out the best in me. You encourage me to be the real me. Something about you spurs me on me to surmount my weaknesses.

Once is quite enough. The audience "gets" it.

Rich characters relay a sense they are real and have a personal history that has made them who they are. You must become your characters when writing a dramatic piece. If your characters are not, in a sense, writing their own dialogue, then it is coming from a false place.

Playwright Tony Kushner says the difference between a good playwright and a bad one is caring about every single word that comes out of a character's mouth. That's why dialogue in dramatic writing has to be discerning.

George Pierce Baker, a Professor of English at Harvard University from 1888–1924, instituted the now legendary 47 Workshop in Drama in 1906. Baker taught, among dozens of students, Eugene O'Neill, Sidney Howard, Thomas Wolfe, and Philip Barry. O'Neill, anxious to join the workshop, wrote Baker: "I want to be an artist or nothing." Entrance standards were extraordinarily high, and admission was granted only to those showing true promise as dramatists. Baker was an icon for me when I entered graduate school as a playwright, armed only with his book *Dramatic Technique*. Writing about dialogue, Baker purports:

> Modern dramatic dialogue had beginnings far from reality. It originated, as the Latin tropes show, in speeches given in unison and to music- a kind of recitative. What was the aim of this earliest dramatic dialogue? It sought to convey, the facts of the episode or incident represented. And that was what good dramatic dialogue has- state clearly the facts which an auditor (audience) must understand if the play is to move ahead steadily... When a dramatist works as he should, the emotions of his characters give him the right words for carrying their feelings to the audience and every word counts... The more real the emotion, the more compact is its expression.
>
> (George Baker's papers can be found in the Harvard Theatre Collection, Houghton Library)

Dialogue can serve the following purposes:

1. Action—moving the plot
2. Characterization and motivation—we can conclude this by what a character chooses to say and what he leaves purposely unsaid.

Characters have two kinds of dialogue always at work. The actual words that come out of their mouths, what they choose to say, comprise the *exterior dialogue*. The *interior dialogue* is what the character is actually thinking and feeling—the subtext. These two kinds of dialogue are as different as cherries and apples. The space between the two is at the heart of most stories. We have to understand characters sometimes say "apples" when their heart is actually feeling "cherries." The writer's work is to discover what is under the disguises, the truth of the characters and their stories. Once we uncover this, we need the courage to confront and expose the truth of each one of them. Explosions often happen at those places where the interior dialogue intersects with the exterior. It's usually the moment where the character can no longer withhold their feelings and they rise to the top.

The following example of feelings rising to the top, so that what is in the character's head and heart finally become text, is from a scene near the end of my play *A Question of Country*, set in South Africa, when Julia and Nabuntu confront each other after they've fought together against apartheid. It is Nabuntu who is exploding from the inside to the outside.

JULIA

I hear De Klerk is in talks.

NABUNTU

They all fart words out their asses.

JULIA

And I know you're hiding guns in your house.

NABUNTU

What's in my house is no longer your business.

JULIA

What did *I* do?

NABUNTU

Oh now you're singing our song. *Senzeni Na, what have I done?* (BEAT) At my house, we're down to the bottom. No mealies, no milk. (BEAT) And you didn't do anything. Our country did.

JULIA

Back *when*, Nabuntu, I came through the fields, and you came running towards me, and we've been together since. My own sister couldn't be more of a sister.

NABUNTU

True. We're Siamese twins; our hearts are attached, but our heads are separate. No matter how you try, Julia, you're still white. Your husband is a big time contractor and my father was in the fishing business. He'd go fishing and sometimes catch something, and we'd eat. But the fishing dried up, and the fish died, and then he died. Still, I'm proud to be descended from Kings and never had to drink black tea or have bread with nothing on it.

JULIA

My parents escaped from Poland; what's happening to your people, happened to my people. Jews and blacks have that in common.

NABUNTU

But at the moment, *you* have the rosy life.

JULIA

Everyone's defecting. Just when we're close to victory in the struggle. I don't understand.

NABUNTU

Because your people are up on a hill in fancy houses with big cars and eating steaks for fine dining at a restaurant with white cloths and flowers on the table and a rich Pinotage from Stellenbosch. The lines are clear a long time. White is good, black is bad, and we won't catch up, even if we win what you call "the struggle." I'm not turning on you; I'm turning back to my own. It's not that you're not appreciated, Julia, but in the end, you're the wrong color for me. You're not black, nieblanke. Some say you use your privileged liberalism only to protect your own status, like "Oh bad apartheid, let us help the poor blacks."

(Shakes her head judgmentally)

JULIA

That's not what I think.

NABUNTU

I have no idea what you think.

JULIA

Both our husbands flew the coop. In *this* way, we *are* the same.

NABUNTU

Only your rooster will come home to claim what's his. Mine has nothing to retrieve ... Try, Julia, but you're not black. I'll open the garage doors and let the Mamas in.

Go through an ordinary day, marking in your journal, hour by hour, what you are doing and what you want. Our "wants" are complex in any one day and are reflected in our dialogue. You wake up and want to go back to sleep, but then you are hungry, then the phone rings and it's someone you don't want to speak to, so now you are both guilty and annoyed, so you distract yourself with the TV and an old movie, but then you are so distracted you are now late for work and consequently are anxious. The range of emotions, even in one hour, is wide. The good news is that all of it is potential material for the writer.

> Parts of this lecture were delivered at New York University's Global Program, "Writing Prague," June 2001

Exercises

1 Write a scene between two characters where intimacy is feigned for opportunistic reasons.
2 Rewrite the following dialogues from well known dramatic works, making it as flat and boring as possible. What makes dialogue boring? Overwriting, repetition, non-specificity, and lack of clarity.

From *Shining City* by Conor McPherson

NEASA: Yeah, well, I didn't … I didn't know that… anything… was… going to happen. I didn't think that there was even anything like that with him… But one day he was…he didn't say anything to me…We just got in the door and I just knew that… what he was…I didn't know what to do. I just, I only kind of realized when we got in the door that…he was…It was just really, I didn't… it was just really quick it was, I didn't even want to do it. We both felt terrible after it. I'm sorry, Ian. I'm sorry. It was only once. It was only one time. It wasn't anything, really. And I've never gone there after.

I'm sorry, Ian.

I don't love him, Ian. I never loved him. I only ever wanted to be with you.

Really. Really.

And I didn't know what happened.

Say something. Say something to me, will you?

From *Good People* by David Lindsay Abaire

MARGARET: I didn't choose to be late. Shit happened, that made me late! Sometimes it was Joyce. Sometimes it was the T. One time I got my car taken. Why'd I lose the car? Because I missed a payment. Why'd I miss a payment? Because I had to pay for a dentist instead. Why'd I have to pay the dentist? Why'd I have to pay the dentist? Because I didn't have insurance, and I cracked a tooth and ignored it for six months, until an abscess formed. Why'd I crack a tooth?

From *Chinatown* by Robert Towne

INT. COUNCIL CHAMBERS

Former Mayor SAM BAGBY is speaking. Behind him is a huge map, with overleafs and bold lettering: "Proposed Alto Vallejo Dam and Reservoir."

BAGBY: Gentlemen, today you can walk out that door, turn right, hop on a streetcar and in twenty-five minutes end up smack in the Pacific Ocean. Now you can swim in it, you can fish in it, you can sail in it -but you can't drink it, you can't water your lawns with it, you can't irrigate an orange grove with it. Remember – we live next door to the ocean but we also live on the edge of the desert. Los Angeles is a desert community. Beneath this building, beneath every street there's a desert. Without water the dust will rise up and cover us as though we'd never existed! (Pausing, letting the implication sink in.)

From *Juno* by Diablo Cody

INT. DRUGSTORE - FRONT COUNTER

JUNO holds the developing test in her hand and slaps the open test box on the front counter. Rollo scans it and bags it indifferently.

JUNO: Oh, and this too.

ROLLO: So what's the prognosis, Fertile Myrtle? Minus or plus?

JUNO (examining stick)

JUNO: I don't know. It's not... seasone yet. Wait. Huh. Yeah, there's that pink plus sign again. God, it's unholy.

She shakes the stick desperately in an attempt to skew the results. Shake. Shake. Nothing.

ROLLO: That ain't no Etch-a-Sketch. This is one doodle that can't be undid.

Taking moments of high emotion in a script, and rewriting them, so the language is flattened out or boring or clichéd, teaches us how *not* to write dialogue.

3 Now, rewrite each of the following three lines to make the language original, spirited, specific, and anything but boring:

I get so angry when you act like that, like you don't even care about me.

I think I'm falling in love with you.

We must *stop seeing each other like this, in secret.*

Assignment

Share your pages, incorporate useful feedback from a critique.

Rewrite the first ten pages, incorporating what you've learned regarding dialogue.

Write the next 15 pages. Now you should have approximately 25 total pages.

Review all 25 pages.

Make certain every line either illuminates character or pushes the plot forward.

Week 4
Escalating conflicts

Keeping the complications moving

Without conflict there is no drama. The Oxford English Dictionary defines conflict as a condition in which a person experiences a clash of opposing wishes or needs. In the typical story the hero/heroine is trying to get something they want and someone else is standing in their way. This is only the beginning of the struggle. Think of the opening conflict as the *situation*, not the plot.

Often, when a student tells me they have run out of plot, as though one could buy it on the shelves of a market, my suspicion is they have failed to escalate the story. What are some examples of escalated plots? The hero, for example, goes in search of his true birth mother. Thinking he's identified her, he bears his heart, only to find that the newly found mother is a scoundrel, collecting personal information from him. She goes on to steal from the hero, leaving him penniless and, in addition, abandoned. The despair brought on by this major disappointment doesn't allow the hero the clear vision needed to recognize his real mother when she does appear. It's said of Raymond Carver's characters in his short stories, or Arthur Miller's in his plays, that they just miss finding their happiness. When using this kind of plot in writing TV comedy, the audience delights when one character keeps screwing up, throwing out the winning lottery ticket and its equivalent in error. This repeated characteristic action then complicates the story and forces the character to try and correct the mistake. Then, using the model of escalating conflict, the correction meant to right things only makes them worse.

In my play *A Small Delegation*, an American professor, Remy, is teaching in Beijing shortly after the end of the Cultural Revolution, and trying to help her translator, Sun, get work in the US. When Sun, after repeated visits to the passport office is denied a passport, Remy decides to intervene. Taking the advice of a seemingly reliable colleague, Remy tries to bribe the passport officer. Not only doesn't it help, but when Sun returns to the office, she is not only denied a passport, but loses her job and is sent to a remote part of China. The colleague who gave the bad advice is later revealed to be a spy. Remy, in meaning to do well and help her Chinese colleague, has ruined her life. That is an escalating conflict.

Did I know all this was gong to happen? When writing the story first as a play, I didn't. For plays I prefer not to know the entire plot, as long as I know the inciting incident and the conflict at the beginning. Then, armed with a strong idea of the characters, I create escalating problems for them and then "watch" how they try to extricate themselves. At every turn they are forced to make a decision, and each decision complicates the plot. We *are* our choices.

When writing a film, because of the multitude of scenes and locations, an outline is a necessity. In this case you are planning the entire screenplay scene by scene and making the characters choose at each turn in the outline. For TV projects you may be handed the scenario and asked to stay tightly within the outline. If you are in a senior position as a writer, you may be given the general idea of the episode and left on your own to figure out how you get there, i.e. the plot.

There is the "mosaic" school of thought, where writers are encouraged to abandon story and just allow a cluster of captivating characters to come together in fascinating settings, letting what happens happen. More often, however, in the successful non-linear piece, audiences are expected to link events and themes, making sense of the story. Sometimes, audiences and critics, fearing to say the emperor has no clothes, confabulate meaning. What makes a good story? The rising tension and danger of what could happen because of the escalating conflicts.

One can do well to go back to Aristotle's *Poetics*, where the author is urged to start at the beginning of the story, where the conflict and situation are laid out. This is your jumping-off point. The film *Witness* begins with a young Amish boy witnessing a murder. It's clear from the outset that the boy, Samuel, has a conflict about reporting it. What's right in his community and society? What's right for him? What might the consequences be? If he does report it, who is put in harm? His mother? Himself? All the escalating conflicts come out of the beginning. If a writer starts too early in the story, he misses momentum gathered from the intensity of the beginning.

One way of adding urgency to the escalating conflicts is the use of a "time lock," which former UCLA professor Lew Hunter discusses in his book *Screenwriting*. The time lock specifies a limited amount of time to solve a problem, as in the films *Forty-Eight Hours* and

High Noon, and it is always present in TV series where there is a murder to be solved by the end of the episode or a problem to be unraveled by the final scene, such as in the recent Netflix series *Grace and Frankie*.

In the first episode, Grace and Frankie's husbands have agreed to reveal that they are lovers, have been for years, and that they are now leaving Grace and Frankie. The tension and comedy incorporate how this news will be divulged and how received, setting up the next episode and the entire series.

John Huston's 1951 film *The African Queen* was adapted from C.S. Forester's novel by Huston and Pulitzer Prize-winning author James Agee (*A Death in the Family*). It is the example I go to first for "escalating conflict "(Chapter 1)." When the German imperial troops, in 1914, burn down a Christian mission and its British leader in Eastern Africa, his sister, the snobbish well-educated Rose, played by Katherine Hepburn, is forced to leave on the only available transport, a thirty-foot dilapidated river boat, piloted by the rough and tumble Charlie Alnut, played by Humphrey Bogart. No odder companions have ever come together, with a huge cultural gulf dividing them. Charlie just wants to wait the war out, quietly drinking. After Rose dumps his entire supply of gin into the lake, she announces her intentions of avenging her brother's death and helping the war effort by building a torpedo and destroying the German warship, the *Louise*, quartered somewhere on this large lake they're sailing down. She convinces a reluctant Charlie and the two are now stuck together for a grueling and challenging trip down Lake Ulana. First, they are shot at by Germans, then attacked by leeches, after which the river dries up and a now bedraggled Rose has to pull the boat through miles of mud, while Charlie steers. Their relief when it starts to rain is short-lived because of the consequent floods. This being Africa, alligators and hippos, real and imagined, raise their heads. There is, however, something good that comes of all the conflict. These two, in fighting the battle side by side, are falling in love. If you've never seen the film, it has a spectacular ending, involving capture aboard the *Louisa* by the Germans, who prepare to hang the two. Only (spoiler alert!), the couple has one last request. They wish to be married before dying. One mystery remains, however. Where is the torpedo they built aboard their small boat, which they've now abandoned? You can guess how they are finally saved.

Why is conflict one of the most difficult challenges for many writers? Maybe it has something to do with our dislike of change. But perhaps it has to do with our unwillingness to confront conflicts. Change, however, is one of the few things we can be certain of, and is usually driven by conflict. We produce art to experience things we don't see or feel in our regular lives. A major question for the writer is the cost of the character's actions when they do confront conflict. Most of us prefer to keep the peace, not ruffle the waters. But that's precisely why you write—to stir things up. The conflicts must force the characters to take action. You are putting the character up against the universe.

With an early workshop of a play at Milwaukee Rep, the then artistic director John Dillon wrote me a long letter listing all the conflicts set out which never went further towards confrontation. It was an early lesson in the lengths we all go to in avoiding stress. A writer friend tells me how he hates confrontation in his life. Then I reflect how that is sometimes a weakness in his writing also. By avoiding confrontation, the conflict remains static, merely a situation without action. Maybe start with confronting in your own life and see what the resulting explosions are. Then, in your own work, CONFRONT.

If you think of escalation as climbing a set of moving stairs, then reaching the top is the climax. Finally, we are brought to a new platform. We are up so high we must move or act. Make certain you know the action of each scene and how it is moving the piece forward. Make an outline of scenes and actions, particularly after your first draft. This is meant as a checkpoint before you start your second draft. Then mark a piece of graph paper, with each square representing one page, and draw a corresponding graph which should mark the escalating conflict slowly making its way upward. In subsequent drafts, identify the highest point in your piece, the action that changes everything and from which there is no going back. If it's not there, put it in.

In TV writing, particularly when you are attempting to sell a new series, much depends on the "pitch." You have to be genuinely excited about the project and gain energy and momentum as you are presenting the story and the character conflicts. You can't fake it. If you lack enthusiasm, what element in the story *would* get you excited? Don't stop until you are sure you have this element in place.

In comedy series as well as dramatic series, we can depend on the quirks of any one character to come into play in how they confront conflict. So the conflicts have to be borne in your original pilot and feed you with enthusiasm. What conflicts and their confrontations will sustain a series? As audiences, we love the certainty in the identification of someone's personality. It's the same way in our lives. We say, "Just you watch how Judy, when she's with you, is always looking around to see if there's a professional or social opportunity in the room. She scans the room and then keeps an eye on the door, seeing who enters, all the while, calculating opportunity. Just watch how she leaps up and insinuates herself." Or, maybe you can count on Tom to always be passive aggressive, so you or the audience can say, "You see. Didn't I tell you what he is like!" This is the same delight in identification of individualities which happens with characters in ongoing series. The audience can depend on what they know about the character. And just when they think they know exactly how any character would act in a particular situation, the character can be tested to see exactly what circumstances may change their usual actions, thus surprising you.

Lecture delivered to the film class at Shanghai Normal University in Xian, June 2015, by Skype

Exercises

1 Take someone you know and identify a predictable, repeated behavior. It should be something you find very annoying. For example, if it is someone very ambitious, when they are with you, they are always looking around to see if anyone "advantageous" enters the space. An advantageous person would be someone who might possibly do something for this person. The character is always looking for opportunity. Don't you wonder what kind of situation will finally trip them up, so they give up the climb? What could possibly stop them from acting in their usual manner? What would finally deter the striving person, forcing them to behave in an unpredictable way?

2 It is now the fourth week of class. Make an outline of the escalating conflicts that will be present in your episode, play, or screenplay. The event in one scene should complicate matters and lead to the next, and so on. It should be a domino effect, even when it is a non-linear piece. Even if you don't end up following the outline, at least you have ballast. You will find that characters often pull you in their own way, something that would be characteristic of this character. Once your character takes on life, you are at the beginning of success, and you will often give in to the character. As a double check, make certain the choice your character is making will complicate the story.

3 Identify the DANGERS in your story so far. Now identify the possible dangers in your outline. If it is not dangerous enough, make corrections.

Assignment

Write the next fifteen pages.

Remember that *drama means action.*

You should now have approximately forty pages if it is a play or screenplay.

If you are writing a shorter episode and have completed your first draft, go back and rewrite, making corrections, including those suggested in the next chapter under "Twenty questions to ask when writing for TV."

Week 5
Sixty questions to ask when writing a dramatic piece

Twenty when writing plays
Twenty when writing screenplays
Twenty when writing for TV

After writing dozens of scripts, it is clear to me the mysterious process of developing a dramatic piece has mostly to do with asking questions. The following are a series of questions I pose at the beginning of a project, all the way through, at the end, and after each rewrite. Most of the character-related questions should be asked at the start of your project. The story, for me, comes from character. What kinds of problems and choices can I give each character that will test them? What will the hurdles be? The thematic questions start being asked towards the middle and thereafter in every rewrite.

No set of rules, especially in a creative medium, can be followed with exactitude. We all know rules are made to be broken. There is no doubt that you can write a strong dramatic piece breaking some or all of these rules. They are, however, helpful as guidelines, a map for the unchartered territory as we write.

Twenty questions to ask when writing a play

1 Who are the characters in your play? Describe them by age, appearance, and temperament. See each physically moving through the play. Describe your characters and cast your play with known actors or with real life people—friends, family, and colleagues.
2 Devise a backstory for each character, including where they grew up, what that was like, major dramatic events in their lives until the moment they walked into your play.
3 Describe the 24 hours in the character's life right before they walked into the first scene. How has that affected their mood, hidden or active?
4 What do they want? Why do they want it?

5 How far will they go to get it? How could this action affect the plot? Choose one of the more dramatic and complex ways.
6 What is the major conflict? Who is standing in opposition to the hero?
7 Who has a secret in your play? What is it? How does it get revealed?
8 Who is clearly the hero or heroine? Remember the hero/heroine has the most to lose in the drama and is the most active. A passive hero does not work. The hero/heroine is always moved to action by the events in the play. What events could move your hero to action?
9 How is your hero changed by the actions in the play? They should be in a different place than they were in the beginning. How has each character changed? What changed them? Their own actions or those of another? If it is a realization, then make the moment active. The audience has to understand what brought about the enlightenment and be present to experience that moment in the play.
10 What are the escalating conflicts? When a play runs out of steam too early it's often because of a lack of *escalating* conflicts (Chapter 4).
11 What are each character's virtues and vices? Are they two sides of the same coin? For example, if a character is generous are they also in danger of giving away too much of themselves and becoming depleted?
12 Describe the physical aspects of your set, visualizing every object that may become significant in the play. What are the predominant colors or color of the set? Once, in a production of one of my comedies, the play had to fight itself across a very dark set. Comedy dictates light colors.
13 What will be the time span of your play? A weekend? A month? A year? How much time do you need to accomplish the journey of this play?
14 What is at stake? This is what keeps the audience engaged. With no stakes, we may be left with only conversation. Another way of asking this question is: what are the dangers? How soon do we recognize them? Does the main character know the dangers up front, or do they escalate due to the character's choices in the play?
15 How does one scene push the next scene forward? If it is a non-linear play, there should be a cumulative action.
16 Is the major action of the play clear? The playwright should be able to state what the play is about in one or two sentences. What you are looking for is focus.

17 What are the critical turning points in the play? When I am considering a director for the project, and have given them the script, I always ask this question. It also serves as a guide for you the writer. You had better have critical turning points in your script!
18 Make certain there is humor in your play. No matter the genre, humor is necessary for relief. What's called for is an understanding of each character's idiosyncrasies and how they can be counted on. For example, the miser will be miserly repeatedly unless he is forced to change. We are all humorous in our humanity and follies.
19 How will your main character change? How will the other characters change? Change is defined by being in a different place than that where you started. What prompted the change? Make sure we see it on stage and not off.
20 What makes *you* return to the writing of this play? Is it that you want to see what happens when you write the next scene? That same returning desire should be present in your audience, especially after an intermission. They should be on the edge of their seats waiting to see what happens. What is the big question at the end of the first act? It's one of the reasons an audience returns after an intermission. What keeps you involved the next time you go to the theater?

Dramatic scripts for theater and film may have the longest journeys. The TV industry is usually quicker in rejecting or giving a green light. The film industry sometimes says "yes," but sometimes ties up the project for several years with rewrites, as the carrot is held out to you. Only the theater is "expert" at having dozens of readings and workshops over many years. The playwright is ever hopeful that one of these will eventually fly. If you know this, it will protect you from being discouraged when you're into your fifth reading. The good news is that this is one of the best ways to get rewrites accomplished, as the play becomes clearer with each reading.

Twenty questions to ask when writing a screenplay

1 Summarize the story you want to tell in a short paragraph. Now shorten it to just a blog line. This will force you to focus the screenplay. Examples of blog lines are:

> *On the Town*—three sailors wreak havoc as they search for love during a whirlwind 24-hour leave in New York City.

North by Northwest—an advertising man is mistaken for a spy, triggering a deadly cross-country chase.

My Brilliant Career—Sybella, a fiercely independent young woman, living in the Australian outback, goes against her family's wishes when she dreams of a career as a writer, and is sent to live with her grandmother, where she is approached by several suitors but in the end turns them all down, deciding marriage is incompatible with her career as a writer.

2 What is the style and tone? Once determined, make certain it is consistent.
3 Who are the major characters? Do short biographies on each, then describe and cast with pictures/photographs, etc. pinned on your wall so the characters are physically always in mind as you are writing.
4 What are the strengths and weaknesses of your major characters? How are these demonstrated in your script? Do they get your character into trouble? How?
5 Why will audiences want to view your film? What makes it exciting? What makes you go to see a film?
6 What do your major characters want? What in their backstories makes them want these things? Think about the major wants you have? What is the source of these wants? When did they begin? Are they from a weakness or strength?
7 Identify your main characters early so the audience knows who the players are and what their major psychological traits are. I like to keep a separate notebook with me, so if I observe someone saying or doing something that reveals everything about him or her, I mark it down. It's how we give away who we are.

Early in my script *Exhibition*, Katie Valentine says:

> I get up every morning and I shake that tree and I say, "Come on day, happen. And if nothing happens, I make it happen. Life's a chef's salad, man. You have to dig in."

The story is about a young woman trying to talk herself into love on a lonely Christmas Eve in New York in the closing hours of the Museum of Modern Art. (Thank you Israel Horovitz for insisting your students write outside the box, not locating plays in living rooms and kitchens. It's a suggestion I never forgot and consequently had me locating plays on the Great Wall of China or in a stadium in South Africa.) She does try and make it happen, but in the end, she can't force the feeling. The story is about thinking you can will something to happen, when you can't.

Another example of a few words that tell us everything about a character is based on a true story. Once I had an event at a major venue in New York, related to a first book publication. When I asked a colleague who shared an office next door, "Are you coming tonight?" he answered as he slammed his office door shut, briefcase in hand, "Nah, I'm outta here." The rudeness and the *screw you* attitude said it all. It was true to character. Thinking about it, it's a lesson that there are sixty ways to say "no."

8 All screenplays are journeys. Where do you want your hero to end up? What would be the most interesting twist? Keep in mind cause and effect. Now construct your storyline scene by scene. In doing so, what will be some of your locations? How will these locations enhance the action of the screenplay?

9 What are the objectives for every character in a scene? Characters enter and stay in scenes because they want something.

10 Where are the dangers in the screenplay?

11 What are the surprises in the screenplay? Are there some that were even surprising to you? Action comes out of whom the person is and how they would act when confronted by choices in the face of trouble.

12 Identify the climax in your storyline. After the climax, nothing should ever be the same.

13 What events brought the story to a climax?

14 When using flashbacks, make certain you are not taking the easy way out of "exposition." Are you sure this is the best way to tell the story? How would the flashback enhance the drama?

15 Make a list of the five films you admire most and why? My five would be *Chinatown, When Harry Met Sally, Pulp Fiction, Midnight Cowboy,* and *Good Will Hunting.* The films all share crisp plotting that is unpredictable. They are films which engage you immediately. You want to know what is going to happen. Happenings are active in contrast to scenes where people are just talking. Always ask what the action of each scene is.

16 Do not use telephone calls if you can help it. The minute I see a phone call in a film, I think "Oh, oh." The screenwriter is doing this for easy exposition. One of the great joys in dramatic writing

is figuring out how you will get important information out without sounding like you are shouting it from a bullhorn.
17 Endings are not the hardest part to write (Chapter 7). For me, the hardest part to write is "the middle." If your middle is sagging it may be because you haven't used enough reversals. Remember, you are challenging the characters and making it hard for them.
18 Do you write a treatment or not? Usually, I plan the plot in a variety of ways. I may first do a scene-by-scene outline. Next I will mark the plot out on a graph so I'm certain of the rising action. Then I will do a treatment. That means you tell the story as a narrative. Perhaps you have occasional dialogue. In a treatment, all the significant characters are present as well as their motivations, in addition to the escalating conflicts (Chapter 4). Always be open to changes in the narrative as you are writing. As you get to know the characters better, they may have minds of their own. All you have to ask is: which way of telling the story is more rousing and dramatic? More active? More electrifying?
19 How do I know when I am finished? After you have done at least four to six rewrites, read it one last time and see if there is anything that can make it better. As a rule, it is cutting. Most writers overwrite. If I get to page 110, I always look to see how far I am from the end. No one wants to read a 150-page screenplay. I know there are examples of screenplays that are this long and sold, but we are looking for the ideal, not the exception. (In reading an already edited draft of a friend's 800-page novel, I found that almost all of it was necessary to the story. So there you are. And it is being published and it will most likely be adapted for film—a long one.)
20 No screenplay prepares you for your next script. You may know all the rules, but the territory is always different. You are an explorer, putting the first footprints onto newly fallen snow.

Twenty questions to ask when writing for TV

1 If this is a pilot, who are the major characters? What are their strengths and weaknesses? What can we expect weekly from these characters in either a comedy or a drama. If it's a comedy like *30 Rock*, the characters usually stay the same. This gives your audiences a kind of comfort zone. They know this character and how they are likely to act and react. So there is predictability about the

people and only the plot is unpredictable. The plot always tests the idiosyncrasies of your characters. In weekly comedies, audiences are watching favorite characters screw up and then make it all come out right in the end. Who usually helps save the major character? Watch old episodes of *I Love Lucy*. Does her husband, Desi, usually save her? Does she save herself by her own wits? Is she just lucky sometimes?

2 If this is a comedy or drama, what makes your central characters likable? For example, in *NCIS New Orleans*, what is it that keeps you tuned in? Is there some way you can always depend on the medical examiner, Dr Loretta Wade, to act? In one episode, while examining the body of a victim seemingly felled by natural causes, she is held hostage in the morgue with her lab tech Sebastian and her young charge Danny. The question is which one of the characters will stand up during the stand-off and what is the unexpected fallout?

3 If this is a pilot for a series, once your major characters are established, what is the trajectory of the story? If it is about someone's downfall, what will be the series of paths? Make a general outline and then go back, filling in the specifics, seeing how you can go from one episode to the next. In the case of *House of Cards*, it is a seemingly downward spiral.

4 In outlining a show with A, B, and C stories, I often use different colored index cards. This makes it easy to discard or shuffle around the story. As a rule of thumb, there are generally twenty-eight scenes in an hour-long episode. The dominant story, the A story, has anywhere from 10–15 beats. The B story can be 7–12 beats and the C story has whatever is left to make up the twenty-eight scenes.

5 Whether a comedy or dramatic series, what does each character think of the other characters? This should be evident from the first episode. These attitudes then feed the plot. For example, if a couple of characters think poorly about another character, expecting them always to fail, then what happens when this same character suddenly wins? You always want the plot testing the characters in any dramatic piece.

6 If you are writing a pilot, outline five possible episodes. Producers are looking for the long-distance runner, a situation that is rich with ongoing possibilities. One time I had gotten very far with pitching a network pilot. It was about a summer camp, with a well-defined supply of idiosyncratic characters and potential for many episodes. In a Hollywood meeting, the network finally

turned it down because they couldn't foresee doing a series that was summer-based and running it in the winter. Well, I did not want to write about a winter camp and so the pilot was put to rest in TV heaven. It's of interest to note that what's not wanted one season may be heralded in another season. Networks make their choices based on last year's popular series or what seems "fresh." The definition of "fresh" also changes with the constantly shifting senior managers and newly hired "hot" executives-in-training. An example of this is the 2015 series *Wet Hot American Summer: First Day of Camp*. It's now considered a nostalgic piece. So if you wait long enough, who knows?

7   Who is your target audience? The demographics for popular TV series keep changing, and just when someone says "The days of the *Golden Girls* are over," along comes Betty White in *Hot in Cleveland*. When you present your ideas you should know the audience you are writing for. Which age range? Which sex? And, the perpetual question in TV, "Will it play in Kansas or Birmingham?"

8   Are there perennial models in television? There are the crime shows with standard plots, dictated by specialty (*Special Victims Unit*) or enhanced by their locations (*NCIS New Orleans*). There are the groups brought together by occupation, friendships, or a common purpose (*The Office, Seinfeld, Glee*). Often there is a "fish out of water" character, especially in a comedy. If the fish gets too comfortable in the water, then your series is over.

9   Try to define what your spec series will be about. Focus it. For example, the series *Everybody Loves Raymond* is about a dependable, solid citizen who gets stuck solving problems for his oddball family and friends. This is also labeled as the *situation*.

10 What is the structure of the usual situation comedy? At the start, the main character is confronted with a problem they must solve. Next, something or someone is standing in their way. This is the *obstacle*. Next, the main character must choose how to try and overcome the obstacle. Often, it is the wrong choice, only he doesn't realize it until it is too late. Next there is an act break, after which the main character suffers the slings and arrows of misfortune caused by his wrong decision. Next, the main character chooses a new approach that turns out only to worsen matters. Last, there is a *resolution* wherein the problem is solved. Often it is something ironic and there was never any problem at all. It's about making a mess.

11 When writing a spec script, the largest dilemma always belongs to the main character. What does your main character want that's in accord with their personality? In the series *Frasier*, for example, the main character is self-important and insecure, so he's always striving to prove himself. He's a social climber and a snob. In your spec episode, what is driving the main character? How is this in line with what the audience knows about the character? Watch weeks of the series and identify what the general premise is every week.

12 In some instances, shows are sold that are a lightly fictionalized version of the real person. An example is *The Jim Gaffigan Show*, developed in 2015 by the cable channel TV Land, owned by Viacom, and starring the comedian with his real-life wife and five kids, all living in a two-room Manhattan apartment on the Lower East Side. In this instance, the writing is based on the author's own life. Jim Gaffigan already had a proven track record on Comedy Central. This show may sound like the series "Louie," but it has one difference: Jim Gaffigan gives you a family show, whereas Louie's character is way out on the edge and over, including language and subject matter. I consider this a late to middle of the night show and one people tend to watch alone. Again, know who your target audience is.

13 The beginning writer who sells a pilot to one of the networks or cable companies should be prepared to fight hard for his right to be a writer on the series. Once you have sold a series it will be easier to get an agent and then hope this agent does battle for you. Be prepared, however, to lose this initial combat. The next time you sell a pilot, you now have a track record and can better demand to be part of the writing team, with a possible producer's credit.

14 Decide what the A story is, then the B, then the C. Each one should have its own log line. This better ensures that there is a conflict or problem to be solved in each of them. Sometimes, when I'm up against a wall thinking up multiple conflicts, I consider some of my friends, or the owner of the new sushi bar where we had dinner last night, or the group of people who are invited for cocktails at a friend's house. Life itself is your best laboratory, so just keep observing.

15 Do you like working quickly and for exceedingly long hours? TV, more than any other dramatic writing medium, demands this. Once you're on board as a writer, you are usually involved

with your writing team and the show runner (head writer) at the helm, outlining and plotting episodes, working with the crew and the director in turning out a season's worth of episodes, usually twelve to fourteen. If the show is successful, more may be ordered.

16 When scripting a pilot spec, identify the genre from the following:

- action/adventure
- comedy (sitcom, satire, sketch comedy)
- drama
- legal drama
- medical drama
- police drama
- medical drama
- science fiction
- daytime drama
- teen drama
- documentary
- unscripted shows, i.e. game show, reality show, talk show, talent show

17 If a comedy or a drama, what are the escalating obstacles in your episode?
18 How will the obstacles be solved? Who solves the problem and how?
19 What moment draws the audience in at the beginning of the episode?
20 What makes your project unique compared to currently airing shows?

Exercises

1 Answer all these questions as best you can at this juncture in your piece. Answer them again at the end of your first draft and after you complete your rewrite.
2 If working on a TV series:
View three current comedy series and three current drama series, identifying the main character's overriding want in each series. The goal of the main character in each episode should be consistent. There's usually a pattern. What is it?

Assignment

Write ten new pages using insights from this chapter.
    You will now have a total of 50 pages.
    Read the first 50 pages aloud with actors and take notes.
    Does anything sound extraneous? Would any scene hold without some of its lines?
    Would any speech read clearer and crisper by cutting some lines?
    Was any section boring?
    Are you saying the same thing twice in any scene? In any speech?
    Remember: lean and mean.
    Is an emotional moment missing?

Week 6
Putting it all together

The making of a play—*A Question of Country* in process

Every script has its own path. Some scripts miraculously get written in one week, in the heat of inspiration, while others take five to ten years to complete. Why? Some of it is the mystery of creativity. There are projects that come to you fully blown, including the characters, the story, and the focus. It has nothing to do with talent. Then there are the 'shape-shifting' stories that come to us piece by problem-solving piece.

In 2002 a story was brought to me as a possible project. It was about a white woman who initiated a grass-roots organization, Ikamva Labantu, during the apartheid years in Cape Town, South Africa. She was working as a nurse on the black side of the Groote Schuur Hospital. The care, as expected in those divided times, was strikingly unequal for black and white.

One weekend the nurse left a seriously ill baby in the ward, but when she returned Monday, the baby had been discharged and reported as "miraculously recovered." Not believing this, the therapist drove out to the black township, a forbidden act in the days of apartheid. She tracked down the "temporary housing" where the mother and baby lived, but the mother, suspecting her of being a spy, at first refused to open the door.

The white woman announced herself as the speech therapist from the hospital, asking through the door how the baby was. "You want to see how my baby is?" the mother finally asked, flinging open the door, revealing a rolled up carpet with her dead baby inside. The two women then drove together to the steps of the hospital, asked to see the chief doctor, unrolled the carpet in front of him, exposing the dead baby. "And this is what your apartheid has done to our country," said the therapist. "I quit."

I was hooked.

It's not that one project is more complex than the other, but rather that with some stories, more and more of the iceberg reveals itself, and at its own pace. You write until you find out what it is you are writing about, batting around a ball of putty until it is as hard as truth. Trust and be patient.

Any story that involves research has to be front-loaded. This may include interviews, reading related books, travel, or combing through archives, and may take six months to three years or more, depending on the amount of material you have to review, as well as your other obligations. This kind of research is also necessarily part of adaptation (Chapter 10), stories based on historical events, and the use of locations and cultures foreign to the writer. Sometimes the subject matter requires further examination, whether you are writing about a group of nuclear scientists or a carnival. Many of us have been instructed to write only about things we know, but I believe we are also meant to stretch ourselves as writers.

When lyricist Yip Harburg wrote the song *April in Paris*, he revealed in interviews that he had never been to Paris. He was then asked how he knew what to write. Yip, lyricist for the film *The Wizard of Oz*, answered, "I've not been *Over the Rainbow* either."

Considering the subject matter of my own plays, I had never been to Las Vegas when I wrote *Almost in Vegas* or had inhabited the body of a Chinese person when I worked on *A Small Delegation*, a play about a group of Americans who come to China to teach in 1987. Nor had I ever been to South Africa when working on *A Question of Country*, about the apartheid and post-apartheid years in Cape Town. Both dramatic pieces were accomplished by research, interviews, and walking in the emotional shoes of the characters.

In *A Small Delegation* there's a scene where a Chinese translator is begging her superior for permission to accept the invitation of a visiting American professor to go to the US on a visiting fellowship. Audiences questioned how, as an American, I understood the "Chinese heart." On reflection, the personal experience of pleading with my own parents to go to college fed the emotional center of that scene. As writers we draw on our memories of how particular emotions felt.

In *A Question of Country*, the white woman, whom I called Julia, was determined to fight against the ruling regime. She ventured into the black townships under cover, building schools, crèches, senior centers, and creating opportunities for the blind, including dancing and training as massage therapists. She also developed hundreds of food programs, continuing these services after the end of apartheid and into the present day.

Putting it all together

Before beginning the project, a meeting was arranged with the woman whom the story was based on. When she came for a meeting from South Africa to New York, we meshed immediately, and with her approval I began work on the play. It was now the summer of 2003, and she generously invited me to stay with her in Cape Town so I could see things first hand and organize interviews.

In preparation, I began by reading *A Country Unmasked* by Alex Boraine, one of the main architects of South Africa's Truth and Reconciliation Commission, and *Country of My Skull* by Antjie Krog (I met Antjie when she came to speak at New York University and, two years later, when we were both recipients of a Rockefeller Grant at Bellagio, Italy). A complete list of the books used in the research for this play appears at the end of this chapter.

The time in Cape Town was a whirlwind of activities. This miracle-making woman was up every morning at dawn, preparing dozens of sandwiches to be delivered to the townships. Then it was into the offices of Ikamva Labantu (The Future of our Nation), staff meetings, and on to the townships and meeting with residents about ongoing problems such as lack of plumbing, medical services, transportation, and the absence of work for both men and women.

It was evident women could only find work as domestics, but most of them lacked training and the necessary "passes" which would allow them to enter the separate "white side" of town. The following is a scene where Julia took matters into her own hands. It's of interest that in a subsequent scene, the therapist steals a pass machine, and that's based on fact.

JULIA

(Runs towards residents with an even larger basket than before)

Need? What do you need?

NABUNTU

Her again.

BOBO

Go away. We know a spy when we see one. (To others) I told you she's cuckoo.

JULIA

(Taking stuff out of her basket)

But, look what I have here. Cheese, salami, come on and smell it. And I have material to make dresses. (Taking out more) Medicine, mealies, and a surprise in my boot.

(She goes to her car. BOBO goes to smell the salami. Seeing JULIA coming back, she drops it. JULIA drags a sewing machine, puts it down. There is dumfounded SILENCE)

I'm going to teach you to sew. Then you Mamas can get jobs.

NABUNTU

(Whispering to BOBO) The woman's a nutcase.

BOBO

(To NABUNTU)

Don't talk to her.

JULIA

(Going on, as if she didn't hear a thing)

We'll make a crèche. I'll show you.

BOBO

(Pointing to NABUNTU) She already made one.

NABUNTU

(To BOBO) Don't talk to her.

BOBO

We've got two babies in the bedroom when her husband's not home.

JULIA

That's just a start. We'll take in many children. Half the township.

NABUNTU

Now I know she's crazy.

JULIA

Not so. We'll find a space. Then, some will take care of children and others will work as domestics. I'll get you passes.

(NABUNTU examines sewing machine, stares at salami) Eat it. Here, take a slice.

(JULIA takes out a pocket knife, slices pieces of salami) You too, come here. (To ZARDIE)

ZARDIE

Do you have cheese sandwiches, lady?

JULIA

Do I have cheese sandwiches? (JULIA unpacks some) Take as many as you want, for your whole family. (ZARDIE takes many sandwiches)

BOBO

Put those sandwiches back, Zardie. (ZARDIE takes a small bite, then puts them back) (To JULIA) Prove you're not a spy.

JULIA

May boils grow on every Boer penis, and trees, forgive me, spring out of their arses.

BOBO

We don't need some fly-by-night. We need work and cabbages.

JULIA

I could get you cabbages.

NABUNTU

You can also get yourself killed. The Kops find you...

ZARDIE

They'll beat you up.

BOBO

And us.

NABUNTU

They say to us, "If you go near the whites, it wrecks the struggle."

JULIA

But I could bring *lots* of cabbages.

NABUNTU

The woman *doesn't* listen.

ZARDIE (As he exits)

I'm going to the road to be a lookout. (To JULIA) Next time, please, park your Julia car outside the highway, near the first robot.

NABUNTU

Not to be rude, but we don't want your cabbages. We prefer to plant our own. I've had five removals. They dump us without water for toilets or washing. I see a six year old dragging around a nine month old in a barrel and I say to myself "Wakee, wakee, Nabuntu."

During the initial visit and two subsequent trips, permission was arranged for interviews with townspeople, members of the Truth and Reconciliation Commission, leading renegades, and those present at some of the major events from 1948 (the beginning of the apartheid movement) to 1991, when DeKlerk started to loosen some of the rules. Other interviews included those present at the Sharpsville massacre, Soweto, the District Six "Removals," and the Cradock uprising, as well as authorities who helped negotiate the release of Nelson Mandela from jail, and were there on that triumphant day in 1990 in Cape Town. Then there were interviews with those on both political sides in the following election years, the victory of the ANC, and research on the post-apartheid years.

One of the most interesting conversations was with Myrtle Berman, an avowed Communist and member of Black Sash, an organization of white women who fought against apartheid. Myrtle told me the story of how she and her husband, Monty, hid Hugh Masekela, the South African musician, in their home and ultimately helped him and Miriam Makeba escape to the US. The way the story was told to me, their house was stormed one night, with the Afrikaner Kops insisting Masekela was hiding under the bed. But all they found was a pair of men's red underpants. Hugh was already gone. They then insisted they were really there to find The Groot Kak (the big shit), meaning Monty Berman. Myrtle and Monty were subsequently arrested, spending two years in jail. While imprisoned, Myrtle fought to get the women prisoners' visitation rights to see their husbands. When she didn't succeed, she organized a hunger strike among the women, until finally, the prison guards relented.

There was more to the story, including the Bermans teaching at the London School of Economics, and I was anxious to include it all in the play. The vast amount of material, however, demanded careful selection for a focused dramatic piece. So, Hugh Masekela's story, along with countless others, had to be omitted. It was a case of having the discipline to "let go of your darlings." Of interest is a 2010 BBC radio documentary, *The Whites Who Fought Apartheid*, featuring Myrtle, who was then eighty-five.

In 2004, I was fortunate to get a Rockefeller Grant to go to Bellagio, Italy. This was a six-week residency, where, without the distractions of everyday life, I settled down to try and make sense of all the research and organize it into the first draft of a drama. No small task.

First, after reviewing all notes, I color-coded them by chronological historical event. Then the interviews had to be typed up and color-coded by character name and corresponding historical event. Next were the decisions about which characters could be combined and reimagined in order to tell the story more dramatically and economically. Then I had to determine who would be the primary characters and what each one of them could possibly "want" in the play. Then I put a cap on the number of characters for practical purposes and decided on six. After all, I wanted the play to get produced!

Later, director Zelda Fichandler, a valued friend from my days in productions at the Arena Stage, remarked that a story of such scope demanded a larger cast. The stage needed to be "peopled." With that advice, I expanded my cast to ten. Did this prevent the play from being widely produced? It did narrow the list of theaters capable of producing it.

Back at Bellagio, settled into a study overlooking Lake Como, I made a glossary as well as a listing of historical events in South Africa from 1948–2000. Then, on a huge piece of cardboard, measuring 48 inches across, I recorded the major events. When finished, I lay the cardboard on the floor and made a storyboard, following the events chronologically, but deciding the story would be told in a non-linear fashion.

After gathering the notes from reading and research, and locating them in time periods, it was time to piece together the possible story, using the major events. In order to shape the piece, I then decided which proceedings could be useful, continuing an ongoing process of selection. This meant eliminating sections of the research. You can compare it to cleaning out a closet and throwing out what you can't use, much as they were once your favorites.

In deciding on a style for the piece, it was clear that the play should be written in a storytelling mode, keeping with African tradition. Next came the task of choosing a narrator. In the end I told the tale through four characters: Julia, Nabuntu, Zardie, and Sipho, with the primary narrators being Julia, the white woman, and Nabuntu, a black townsperson who joins forces with her. In the end, the play was centered on Nabuntu.

An example follows of the storytelling mode at the beginning of the play:

A BARE STAGE. TABLE MOUNTAIN IS IN THE BACKGROUND. LIGHTS COME UP, NABUNTU ENTERS.

NABUNTU
(Entering)

If you asked me if I would let Julia into my life, if I had it to do again, I don't know. You'd have to read history and figure out how we came to be the ones without, and others, like Julia, had it all. At the time we needed someone to pull us up. Some say, "Only the privileged can afford to give charity."

JULIA
(Entering from the opposite side)

I could always smell need like tiger smells meat.

ZARDIE
(Entering)

Nabuntu and Julia? At one time, they were joined at the hip.

SIPHO

Those two? They were the eyes of the needle, and those of us who didn't like how our country was going, threaded ourselves through them, to turn things.

JULIA

Nabuntu was like a big wind. To make fire, you need wind. We were thrown in the trenches together, into the thick of it.

NABUNTU

You could say we threw *ourselves* in. Julia came to us like some kind of want-to-be angel. The first time I met her, she comes running out of a field, from nowhere. "Need, need?" she's calling to me. I think this woman is cracked. No whites allowed here.

The real "Julia" insisted she didn't want the story to be about her, but in the writing, that character kept pulling the story away from the others. The problem was I didn't want this to be a Joan of Arc story, with the white woman as the heroine. At the start, it was the white woman who organized all the blacks in the townships, readying them to do the work independently. In the first draft this Mother Teresa aspect was still there, but I wanted to honor all the people who worked together.

The first reading was done in March 2006 at the McCarter Theatre in Princeton, New Jersey, under the artistic direction of Emily Mann. It featured the splendid Myra Taylor as Nabuntu and Liesel Tommy, a South African actress, now turned director. Emily Mann suggested a young South African, Barbara Rubin, as the director. As in most readings, we rehearsed all day, presenting the play late in the afternoon. As sometimes happens, despite its good reception, Emily decided not to go further with the project. She was artistically engaged at the time, she told me, with playwright Athol Fugard, and felt her first loyalty was to him and his work.

That reading, as it turned out, was an opportunity to rewrite and change some of the things I felt weren't working. Besides not wanting Julia to be the solitary heroine, the story needed to be more dramatic in terms of escalating conflicts. But here was the problem: in order to tell the story and remain true to the facts, my hands were tied behind my back. It was clear I would have to change some of the particulars to make the play work.

To begin with, it didn't make sense that Julia's husband would stay and tolerate the pandemonium in the household. If I could only have Julia taking more and more chances and have the husband get fed up and leave, the stakes would be higher. Then there was a blind character I had interviewed. He was referred to as Blind Martin and I kept that name. But the writer is always propelled by "what if?" So, I thought, "What if, in the play, Julia encourages Blind Martin to help her build a school—a forbidden act. Then, being anxious to please Julia, Martin would carry on construction at night, after Julia left the township. Then what if the police discovered and arrested him, and it had dire consequences, ending in Julia's arrest? That could be the end of Act 1. But this was all based on "what ifs" and not the true story. My only choice in heightening the drama was to ask the woman Julia was based on if I could change things slightly.

So, I wrote to her in South Africa, explaining the dramatic dilemma. In very short time, a surprising answer came back. She agreed with the taking of dramatic license for two reasons. First, she acknowledged there were several grass-roots organizations in South Africa during apartheid, and she didn't want to call attention just to the one she had started. They all shared equally in the work. Relieved, I suggested dedicating the play to Ikamva Labantu and the many other grass-roots organizations that participated in the fight, which I did. Second, she agreed some of the people interviewed wouldn't understand if their real story was combined with two or three more true stories. In the end, the title changed from *Ikamva Labantu* to *A Question of Country*. Underneath the title were the words "Based on a true story."

With the date of the next workshop, sponsored by The Culture Project in New York, set for 2008, I went to work on the next draft. Zelda Fichandler suggested Benny Ambush as a director for the project. We met, he "got" the play, and all was in motion. The rewrite was extensive, now including the arrest of Julia, a separation between her and her lawyer husband, her instigation of the building of a school by a blind township boy, and extensive cuts of sections that detracted from the focus of the main story, including the deletion of any parts which felt didactic and more like a "history lesson."

Armed with a rewritten script and a cast, with Myra Taylor as Nabuntu again, there was one rehearsal and then a reading at the Barrow Street Theatre in Greenwich Village. The rewrites worked, the cuts worked, and I now had a far better script. A few months later, the Artistic Producing arm of the Culture Project agreed it was an exciting piece, but they couldn't produce the play now because it wasn't an authentic documentary, like their successful production of *The Exonerated*. With one organization, then, "based on" turned out to be a detriment.

Something still bothered me in the script. In the process of readings and rewrites there was a discovery about the very center of the play. It's the old onion metaphor, where you are peeling more and more before you get to the core. Maybe what the play was about was the improbability of ever crossing the class/economic divide? In post-apartheid, the whites were still living in houses on top of a hill and dining in restaurants with white tablecloths, while in the townships, life was essentially unchanged. At heart, it was about the slowness of change and the impossibility of the friendship between Julia and Nabuntu in post-apartheid South Africa. Like soldiers fighting in wartime, they were once like sisters, but the fight was over now, and the race/class divide in their two lives was impassable.

After a fourth draft, my agent sent the play to a reputable Broadway producer, who, after reading the script, called to set up a meeting. The producer turned out to be genuinely enthusiastic and dramaturgically astute. After a lengthy discussion, I agreed to look at some questions the dramaturgs in her office raised, attend to them, and recontact her. Six months later, with the next rewrite completed, we met again. It now seemed, however, that those same dramaturgs felt the rewrites I had done raised more questions than they answered. Also, in the interim, the producer was knee deep in a new Broadway production about Africa, and so my play was no longer at the top of her list. Few things match the eternal optimism and determination of the playwright. So I waited, and on next contact, she wrote back that she regretfully had too much on her plate presently.

It was at this juncture that the head of the directing program at a college theater department in Boston wanted to do two workshops, six months apart, using local actors, including the splendid Robbie McCauley playing Nabuntu. We did a read-through in November, there were a few rewrites, and a workshop was scheduled for the late spring, with an invited audience, including Boston theater producers. It should be noted the play had now gone through numerous workshops and was in excellent shape. This never means your work as a playwright is finished, but only that it is closer to a final and producible draft.

The spring workshop did not go well for a multitude of reasons. In theater, film, and TV, there are a hundred reasons why a project can go poorly. But just when you think you have experienced every one of them, number 101 rears its head. Let that suffice.

After that, a giant sinkhole emerged. One has those periods where one feels beaten and ready to pursue a career as a landscape gardener or a beauty consultant in the cosmetics department of Bloomingdales. It's not uncommon to contemplate leaving the profession periodically (as in "Who needs this?"), but the usual trajectory is the slough of despond, until you eventually lift yourself out of it because you can't help yourself. You've chosen to be a writer and the bug will never leave you. The only cure is getting back to your desk.

Next, you either decide to write a novel or reframe the play as a screenplay—or you start a new play, or you meet with your agent, figuring out what theaters have rejected the piece and which theaters remain. Maybe you even send the manuscript a second time to places that originally rejected it, but with a new title. After all, if enough time has passed, there could be new readers.

In spring of 2010, I was speaking with Leslie Lee, an incredible man and playwright, now sadly departed. When I told him the saga up to that moment and the uphill struggle, he asked to read the play. He was then in charge of new projects for Negro Ensemble Company (NEC), an established black theater company in New York. The script called for a large black cast. Perfect.

Leslie sent the play to director Ricardo Khan at Crossroads Theatre, we all met, and a reading was scheduled for September 2011. There would be two rehearsals. It looked promising. Ricardo understood clearly what I was writing and that Nabuntu, the black woman, was telling the story from her point of view. By that time, the script was tight, and all that was needed was some small trimming. It came in at 93 pages and would run approximately two hours. Patricia McCorkle, the casting agent, was spot on and moved quickly. When it turned out actress Roslyn Ruff had a conflicting TV commitment, they came up with numerous new suggestions. The final cast included Irungu Mutu, Okwui Okpokwasili, Maaneyaa Boafo, Avery Glymph, and Yaegel Welch.

With this strong cast, Ricardo focused the play clearly, stamping it with his personal vision. He insisted we have a harp, rehearsed the actors in the Gumboot dance, introduced South African music, and after the two rehearsals, we were ready to go.

But, by this time, NEC was struggling financially, and on the date of the reading, Leslie warned me NEC's future was bleak. They were now unable to secure their usual space, and we would have to use a rented space on West 43rd Street. In truth, my heart went out to them, as the death knoll was tolling for this magnificent theater company. Leslie was clear in emphasizing a future production could not be promised. Being a writer for the theater, this was not new to me. Onward. It was now ten years since I started writing this play.

The audience was filled, the workshop was successful, but who could have predicted the hottest night in September in history, and the air conditioning was broken on the fifth floor of a rented space on 43rd Street. After that, NEC was in continuous financial struggle, only managing to present a few readings, fundraisers, and the occasional subsidized production. It's cheering to note that Signature Theatre in New York subsequently did an entire season of work from NEC playwrights. Bless their artistic director, Jim Houghton.

When someone suggested Niegel Smith might be the right director, the play was sent to him, and his quick response of "I have to do this play and let's meet" led to one of the most inventive and original directors yet. His grasp of *A Question of Country* and his production ideas lit me on fire. Finally, I had my director. Niegel brought the project to the attention of theaters from Oregon Shakespeare to Mixed Blood, but some artistic directors were hesitant to do a play about South Africa by a white woman, and one from America to boot. Some just couldn't do this large a cast. This was becoming a long and discouraging journey for such a "promising" play. Niegel Smith was appointed Artistic Director of the Flea Theater in New York in 2015.

There was yet one more workshop at Theater for The New City in New York followed by one at Queens College. At this juncture it was gratifying just to have good actors put it out there. Did I think this workshop process might go on for the rest of my professional life? Yes. The play seemed to be in a loop of development.

The other day, a new theater was in contact, and is considering *A Question of Country*. The artistic director asked me to be patient. At this stage would patience be a virtue or a place to hide? In the theater, no one knows anything for certain. But I do remember August Wilson telling me he had ten readings of *The Piano Lesson* before it was produced, and it was said that Sarah Ruhl had thirteen readings/workshops of *The Clean House* prior to its first production.

Is there a lesson in all this? There is. The development process of any project is unique. Expect the unexpected. Like the writing, some production experiences take a week to solidify and some take years. Yet others, despite having successful development, never move on to full production.

I've learned all of it is part of your professional fabric, contributing to the whole. The entirety consists of stories you may not use, ones that go belly up never taking on life, those that do go on but fail, those that take ten years of workshops, and then the ones that triumph, are produced, and finally your tummy is full—until it's empty again. So, you start a new project. As writers we are always "in process."

Exercises

1 Draw up a plot plan scene by scene so you are in control of your project. Remember this is only an idea of what you think is going to happen. If the action changes because a character's true self is taking over, have the courage to change that outline, or to figure

out exactly how you will get from point A to point B, as delineated in your outline. Make sure the plot is true to your characters and their complexities. We all have buttons that get pushed which leads us sometimes to uncharacteristic actions, and the accompanying consequences.

Assignment

Rewrite pages 1–25 or the first half if it is a TV script. This may be your second rewrite if you have answered and corrected some of last week's work.

Refer to Chapter 9 on rewriting.

For the following week, rewrite the second half of your project if it is for TV. Rewrite approximately pages 25–50 or the end of a scene that is nearest page 50.

Bibliography for *A Question of Country*

Boraine, Alex (2000), *A Country Unmasked: Inside South Africa's Truth and Reconciliation Commission*, Oxford University Press.
Cahill, Kevin (1993), *A Framework for Survival: Health, human rights and humanitarian assistance in conflicts and disasters*, Council on Foreign Relations.
Coles, Robert (2000), *Lives of Moral Leadership*, Random House.
Finnegan, William (1986), *Crossing the Line: A year in the land of apartheid*, Harper & Row.
Fugard, Athol (1984), *Notebooks, 1960–1977*, Alfred Knopf.
Gallagher, Winifred (1994), *The Power of Place: How our surroundings shape our thoughts, emotions, and actions*, Harper Perennial.
Gobodo_Madikizela, Pumla (2002), *A Human Being Died That Night*, Houghton-Mifflin.
Hayner, Priscilla (2001), *Unspeakable Truths: Confronting state terror and atrocity*, Routledge.
Human Rights Watch (2001), *Scared at School: Sexual violence against girls*, Human Rights Watch.
Kaplan, Robert (1996), *The Ends of the Earth: A journey to the frontiers of anarchy*, Random House.
Krog, Antjie (1998), *Country of My Skull: Guilt, sorrow, and the limits of forgiveness in the new South Africa*, Three Rivers Press.
Levine, Janet (1988), *Inside Apartheid*, Contemporary Books.
Malan, Rian (1990), *My Traitor's Heart*, Grove Press.
Mandela, Nelson (1994), *Long Way to Freedom*, Little, Brown & Co.
Miller, Sarah (1927), *The South Africans*, Boni and Liverwright.

Rasebotsa, Nobuntu and Molema, Leloba (eds), *Women Creating the Future: An anthology of women's writing in South Africa*.
Richmond, Simon and Murray, Jon (2002), *Cape Town*, Lonely Planet Publications.
Rive, Richard (1986), *Buckingham Palace District Six*, David Philip.
Slovo, Gillian (1997), *Every Secret Thing*, Little, Brown & Co.
Tutu, Desmond (2000), *No Future without Forgiveness*, Doubleday.
Vassen, Robert D. (ed.) (1999), *Letters from Robben Island: A selection of Ahmad Kathrada's prison correspondence*, Zebra Press.
Wolpe, Annmarie (1994), *The Long Way Home*, Virago Press.

Week 7
Endings

What can an ending accomplish?
How do you know when you are there?
Avoiding the three-ending script

When I asked a group of writers what was the most difficult task in writing a dramatic script, unanimously they answered, "Endings!" And so, I decided to investigate the qualities that combined to formulate a successful ending.

The Oxford English Dictionary defines an ending as follows: an action that concludes, completes, or terminates. It is also described as a boundary, an outcome, a result, a final purpose, the object for which the thing exists, the direction in which one wants to play towards, as in the end zone, and as a destination.

The ending of a play or screenplay is the very last image, as well as the very last spoken word. Israel Horovitz, who was my teacher at Brandeis, instructed his students to note the last word in their scripts and determine if there was any significance in that word or sound. Did it connect with the question the piece was asking or the conflict it was attempting to resolve? Two widely quoted endings in film are in *Casablanca* and *Gone With the Wind*: Rick's "I think this is the beginning of a wonderful friendship, Louis"; and Rhett Butler's answer to Scarlett's "If you go, where shall I go?" when he finally abandons any continuing responsibility for Scarlett's manipulations—"Frankly, my dear, I don't give a damn." These are ideal resolutions for the main questions of those films.

A film of 2015 by Zhang Yimou, *Coming Home*, leaves the viewer with a haunting image. At the end of the Cultural Revolution, a woman awaiting the return of her husband shows signs of encroaching dementia. By the time the husband returns, she fails to recognize him, thinking him a stranger. When she locks the returned husband out, he finds a flat next door. Every day for years, as her dementia worsens, he visits, establishing a friendship, even reading aloud to her the letters he sent to her while he was away. One of the letters says he will arrive home on the eighteenth of the month. Thereafter, the woman comes to the train station on the eighteen of every month and waits, accompanied by her new friend next door (actually her husband), holding a large "Welcome home" sign. Every time the train empties, the passengers come down a flight of iron stairs to be greeted by friends and families, but the husband the woman is waiting for is never there. The irony is he is there all along, being her new best friend. In the last scene, with snow falling, the two of them are now quite old and he takes her to the train station by a wagon he pulls. They wait and wait as always, but in vain. The snow is falling on them. There is no music, not a sound, as the snow gets heavier and they fade out of view, waiting silently. This last image says it all. If you were a writer and this scene was written by you, it seems to me you could then die happily.

In a 2015 TV series, *Blindspot*, a beautiful woman, temporarily named "Jane Doe" and covered with tattoos, mysteriously appears out of a zippered bag in Times Square, without any knowledge of her past. The only identification is a tag urging the finder to contact the FBI. When special agent Weller is called in to solve the case, he discovers his name is one of the tattoos on the woman's back. The clues to the case are in the tattoos. Most every tattoo is a warning of forthcoming danger, which he tries to stop. If Weller is Batman then Jane Doe is his Robin, as they piece together the jigsaw puzzle of her life, week by week. They discover she can speak Chinese and probably had been involved in martial arts, and they guess she was a Navy Seal. Agent Weller sets her up in a safe house. She then depends on Weller for her only comfort, and he needs her as well, for her martial-arts skills. In their own way, both are kind of lost souls and become dependent on each other.

Each episode ends with them thwarting a new danger, piecing together another part of the mystery, and becoming closer. Romance is inevitable, of course. Do I fault the writers and female producers for this? Not at all. Their business is to keep their audience interested and preserve the future of the show.

Piper Chapman is a public-relations executive with a career and a fiancé in *Orange Is the New Black*, a Netflix series. Piper's past suddenly catches up to her in her mid 30s, when she is sentenced to spend time in a minimum-security women's prison for her association with a drug runner ten years earlier. Clad in prison orange, like her prison mates, Chapman starts off behaving as if she were at a tea party. Each week, however, forces her to toughen up, in order to make her way through the corrections system and adjust to life behind bars. In an early episode, she denigrates the prison food, not knowing she is speaking to the head of the kitchen, Rosa. When Rosa then serves Piper a used tampon on a bun, followed by no food at all, Piper has to figure out how to get back on Rosa's good side (if there is one) and get fed. The other inmates are Black, Asian, Latino, and White, and all eccentric, including a former nun, a schizophrenic, a self-appointed preacher, and "Crazy Eyes." Piper's stay is complicated when her former lesbian lover, the drug dealer, is incarcerated in the same prison. Much lesbian lovemaking is the music of the showers in this more-than-edgy series. As Piper hardens in order to survive, each episode presents a new problem to be solved, concluding with her continuing education. At the end of the fourth season, there's a joyous episode where all the inmates go on an outing, find a lake, and jump in jubilantly. Piper is a fish out of water when she enters the prison, but becomes a piranha.

Playwright John Guare, when asked if he wrote with endings in mind, told an interviewer:

> If you knew where you were going why would you bother writing? There'd be nothing to discover. I can still remember throwing up when I realized what the ending of *The House Of Blue Leaves* would be—that after Artie the songwriter realized the true worth of his work he would have to kill his wife because she saw him as he was.

In a production of Bryony Lavery's play *Last Easter* (2004) off-Broadway, the character Gash, played by actor Jeffrey Carlson, calls after his friend June, who has just died from cancer and departed into the "afterlife" by walking down the theater aisle out through the audience: "Is there anything out there?" And he repeats it. It's the final sound of faith being questioned, and because faith is the comic underbelly of this play, the call into the void is all the more wrenching. It completes the journey of the cynical faithless that want something after all—call it faith or God, or God spelled backwards, as evidenced in the last line of the play, which circles back to the convention of jokes used throughout. In this way the author states the case for faith, and at the same time questions it. The play appears to be a comedy about a group of friends supporting a friend through her last days of cancer, but it turns ever so gently at the end, kicking you in the heart, and it is a wipeout.

In examining endings, we should look to fairy tales as models. In the fairy tale there is generally a difficulty that has to be solved, whether it is the wolf that has devoured Little Red Riding Hood's grandmother, or Sleeping Beauty, who can only be woken by a kiss from a prince.

When that problem, or the evil, is confronted, the story can come to its conclusion, which means a change of circumstances, and therefore, a closure.

In the conclusion to his book *Readings for the Plot*, Peter Brooks states that narrative is one of the ways in which we think and speak, and "plot is its thread of design and active shaping force, the product of our refusal to allow temporality to be meaningless, our stubborn insistence on making meaning in the world and in our lives."

It is in our endings that we find the meaning in our scripts, and this meaning only shows its face to the writer at the completion of the writing journey. When you are closer to knowing what question you are asking in your piece, you are closer to writing an effective ending.

Arthur Miller, in his essay on "The Family in Modern Drama," says it is content which dictates form, and so no rules about endings can be applied mechanically. For me, this is a central joy in writing—figuring out the individual architecture for each piece. This is essentially true for plays, films, TV episodes, short stories, novels, essays and poems. In the same essay, Miller says:

> Most people have come to assume that the forms in which plays are written, spring either from nowhere or from the temperamental choice of the playwrights. I am not maintaining that the selection of the form is as objective a matter as the choice of let us say a raincoat instead of a linen suit for a walk on a rainy day; on the contrary, most playwrights, including myself, reach rather instinctively for that form, that telling of a play, which seems inevitably right for the subject at hand.

And so it is with endings. When you are coming to the conclusion of your dramatic script, you are a chariot driver with many reins in your two hands; and, as you near the finish of the race, you hold tighter and tighter onto these reins, so that they all knot into one.

What are these reins? You are holding in your hands all the narrative threads. When we speak about a writer "earning an ending" we mean that the ending should be organic to the narrative line of the piece.

Sometimes I go back over a dramatic script and diagram the narrative development for each character. Then, I diagram the accompanying emotional chronology for each character. Next, I diagram the action of the play, the plot, from beginning to end. Then I go back to the original question the play is asking and see if that through-line of the question follows in the script.

When these complex threads are outlined, I put them up on a wall or down on any flat surface, so I can review the scope of what I'm writing. Then I commit these various threads to memory and walk with them for a while. You want to make certain that you've followed through on all the lines of your story. Now, holding these lines as reins, as a chariot driver, draw them tighter and tighter to your chest until the final image is forged between your two hands. Many times, this final image just comes to you when you are doing something else—walking in the park, taking a shower, riding on the subway. This image evolves seemingly mysteriously, but it works it way out of the subconscious much as a baby chick breaks out of an egg.

We should examine the following endings in order to see what works.

In Conor McPherson's play *Shining City*, which opened at the Royal Court Theatre in London in the summer of 2004, and takes place in Dublin, a man comes to a therapist seeking help. He claims to have seen the ghost of his recently deceased wife.

> I was just going into the living room and I put the lights on, and... when I turned around I could see that she was standing there behind the door looking at me... her hair was soaking wet, and all plastered to her face... I mean it's unbelievable, you know... well finally, I don't know how, but I just got my legs going and went straight out the door, straight by her... she was behind it.

The man describes the ghost of his wife as being dressed in red. In the course of the play, the therapist "cures" the man, taking his red-dressed ghost away from him. The therapist has his own problems, which his patient "outs." The final moments of the play follow. The therapist is Ian, and his patient, now cured, is John.

IAN

I think you had a real experience. I think you really experienced something—but I think it happened because you needed to experience it... you were pulling all this... you felt maybe you couldn't move on without being... punished somehow... it happened! BUT... I don't believe you saw a ghost. Does that make sense?

JOHN

Well, yeah, it makes sense to me now. But there was a time it really wouldn't have, you know? But that was a different time.

IAN

Yeah, it was.

JOHN

... I'll see you.

IAN

I'll wait here till you get out down there.

JOHN

I'll see you Ian, good luck.

IAN

I'll see you, John, bye now.

(IAN hovers near the open door while JOHN goes down. We hear the outer door slam shut. IAN calls out...)

Did you get out?

(There is no answer. IAN shuts the door and crosses the room. In the darkening gloom of the afternoon, we see that the ghost of John's wife has appeared behind the door. She is looking at IAN, just as JOHN described her; she wears her red coat and her hair is wet. She looks terrifying. IAN has his back to her at his desk, going through some papers. But he seems to sense something and turns)

(Lights down)

This is one of the most memorable endings in contemporary dramatic literature. For me it's about how we listen to another's problems so intently sometimes, we inherit them, as we free the storyteller. Also, it depicts two men trying to help each other in a struggle between the living and the dead. One goes off cured, as he hoped, and the other inherits the ghost in red.

Lorraine Hansberry's *A Raisin in the Sun* refers to a Langston Hughes poem, *Dream Deferred*.

What happens to a dream deferred?
Does it dry up?
Like a raisin in the sun?
Or fester like a sore—

And then run?
Does it stink like rotten meat?
Or crust and sugar over—
Like a syrupy sweet?
Maybe it just sags
Like a heavy load.
Or does it explode?

In *A Raisin in the Sun*, the Youngers, a struggling black family living in Chicago in the 1950s, inherit $10,000 in insurance money from their deceased father, and decide to purchase a house in a white neighborhood. As the family packs, a representative from the neighborhood, Carl Lindner, comes with a proposal: the Clybourne Park Neighborhood Association will pay the Youngers *not* to move in. The family refuses. However, when Walter Lee, the supposed head of the household, loses $6,500 of the insurance money in a venture to open a liquor store, he says he will allow the family to be bought out. He says, "You know it's all divided up. Life is. Sure enough. Between the takers and the taken."

Walter Lee is tired of falling into the latter category. His sister, Beneatha, swears if he kneels to the powers that be, he will no longer be her brother; and their mother, Lena (the *actual* head of the household), chastises Beneatha:

> Child, when do you think is the time to love somebody the most? When they done good and made things easy for everybody? ... That ain't the time at all. It's when he's at his lowest and can't believe in hisself 'cause the world done whipped him so!

Soon after that, Lindner arrives again, ready to pay the Youngers off—however, Walter Lee defies everyone's expectations, saying,

> We have decided to move into our house because my father—my father—he earned it for us brick by brick. We don't want to make no trouble for nobody or fight no causes, and we will try to be good neighbors. And that's all we got to say about that. We don't want your money.

As soon as Mr. Lindner is gone, the family returns quickly to the frenzy of moving, attempting to ignore the nobility of Walter's action. After everyone is gone, we see Mama, alone in the apartment she's raised her children in:

(MAMA stands, at last alone in the living room, her plant on the table before her as the lights start to come down. She looks around at all the walls and ceilings and suddenly, despite herself, while the children call below, a great heaving thing rises in her and she puts her fist to her mouth to stifle it, takes a final desperate look, pulls her coat about her, pats her hat and goes out. The lights dim down. The door opens and she comes back in, grabs her plant, and goes out for the last time)

The final moment of the play with Mama encapsulates the struggle of the mother for acceptance of her family's place in society, and the family's defiance of the housing restrictions, threats, and bribery, all meant to keep the present social order intact. Lorraine Hansberry, relating the lessons her parents taught her that later influenced the play, said, "We were the products of the proudest and most mistreated of the races of men... above all, there were two things which were never to be betrayed, the family and the race." The play is dedicated "To Mama: *in gratitude for the dream.*"

The play is about the quest for a dream. The Youngers do get their dream. They will move to the house in the all white neighborhood. But there is a price for the acquisition of that dream, and for their disruption of the status quo. *A Raisin in the Sun* premiered on Broadway in 1959, in the midst of the Civil Rights Movement, and as such, represents choices that had to be made by an entire generation. The play, although highly personal, relates to the entirety of the 1960s and civil liberties. The Youngers' fight became everybody's fight. The dreams of the Civil Rights Movement were not achieved without a price. Mama is all of us, trying to get out.

What does Hansberry accomplish with the silence of the play's final moment? One interpretation is that Mama stares the future in the face, knows it is uncertain, both the victory and the knowledge of the struggle ahead. She takes one last look around her house, gets dressed in her armor of coat and hat, opens the door, doesn't slam it, and comes back in for the last to grab her plant. She is taking both the remnants of the past and the possibility of growth in the future.

In Wendy Wasserstein's comic drama, *The Sisters Rosensweig*, a different kind of family play, we watch three Jewish sisters from Brooklyn gather at the eldest's house in Queen Anne's Gate, London. They all have strayed far from their roots, though the middle daughter, Gorgeous, has done basically what was expected of her: she married a lawyer, had kids, moved to the suburbs of Boston, and is leading the women's group from her synagogue on a tour of London.

The play deals with the complex relationship between what these women are looking for and what they actually have, as well as their distance from each other and their past. The play opens with the eldest sister's daughter, Tess, listening to a recording of her mother, Sara, singing in an a capella group at college; she's doing a biography of her mother's early years for a school project. "It's pretentious," Tess says as the play begins. Though singing was clearly an important part of Sara's past, she refuses to sing throughout the play... until its closing moments. Gorgeous has just gone to return the Chanel ensemble the women's group has given her as a thank-you gift so she can pay her kids' tuition. Pfeni, the youngest, has gone to Tajikistan to write the book she's always meant to, and Sara has just said goodbye (maybe temporarily, maybe not) to the new, older, and very sensible man in her life. Finally alone with her mom, Tess asks Sara for an interview for her school project.

SARA

My name is Sara Rosensweig. I am the daughter of Rita and Maury Rosensweig. I was born in Brooklyn, New York, August 23, 1937.

TESS

And when did you first sing?

SARA

I made my debut at La Scala at fourteen.

TESS

Mother!

SARA

I first sang at the Hanukah Festival at East Midwood Jewish Center. I played a candle.

TESS

And why did you become a Cliffe Clef?

SARA

You great-grandfather thought I could be a singer.

                    TESS

Would you sing something now?

                    SARA

Honey, it's so early.

                    TESS

Please sing something. *Begins to sing.*

Shine on, shine on, harvest moon
Up in the sky.

                    SARA

I ain't had no loving since January, February, June, or July.

                    TESS

Do it, mother!

                    SARA

Snow time ain't no time to stay outdoors and spoon.

              TESS and SARA

So shine on, shine on, harvest moon.

(SARA *sings, touching her daughter's face*)

For me and my gal.

In this simple gesture, we see, finally, a hard won moment of pure connection between mother and daughter, past and present. While we know these characters will continue to struggle, a small understanding and bond has been accomplished.

The Sisters Rosensweig owes a great deal to Chekhov's *The Three Sisters*. Its ending, however, doesn't leave us with the same tender glow. Olga, Masha, and Irina spend the entire play looking for a way to escape their provincial existence and return to their hometown, Moscow. Like Sara, Gorgeous, and Pfeni, they are living in a present in which all connections to their past have disappeared; but unlike the sisters Rosensweig, these women are not trying to escape their past, but rather return to it. When the handsome captain Vershinin comes to town and they realize that they knew him in Moscow, he immediately becomes a constant guest in their home and inspires vivid dreams of a return to the city. However, as it often is in Chekhov and in life, nothing goes according to plan. By the end of Act 4, Irina's fiancée, Tuzenbach, has been shot in a duel, all the soldiers are leaving, and Natasha, their sister-in-law, has declared their favorite orchard of cherry trees, outside the family home, will be cut down to make way for new housing. After the discovery of Tuzenbach's death, the sisters are left alone with the retired army doctor, Chebutykin. They listen to the music of the departing soldiers.

MASHA

Oh, listen to the music! They're going away. One of them has already gone away for good. We're alone, and now we have to start our lives all over again... we have to go on living...

IRINA

Someday everyone will know what this was all about, all this suffering—it won't be a mystery anymore—but until then we have to go on living... and working, just keep on working. I'll go away tomorrow, by myself. I'll teach school and devote my whole life to people who need it... who may need it. It's autumn, winter will come, the snow will fall, and I will go on working and working.

OLGA

The music sounds so happy, so positive, it makes you want to live. Oh, dear God. The day will come when we'll go away forever too. People will forget all about us, they'll forget what we looked like and what our voices sounded like and how many of us there were, but our suffering will turn to joy for the people who live after us, their lives will be happy and peaceful, and they'll remember us kindly and bless us. My dears, my dear sisters, life isn't over yet. We'll all go on living. The music sounds so happy and joyful, it almost seems as if a minute more, and we'd know why we live, why we suffer. If only we knew. If only we knew!

(The music grows softer and softer)

CHEBUTYKIN

(Singing softly) Ta-ra-ra-boom-de-ay, it's going to rain today... (Reads his newspaper) What difference does it make? What difference does it make?

OLGA

If only we knew! If only we knew!

Endings

Even as the sisters' hope of change in their situation ebbs away, they are resolved to continue their lives as they have always lived them. This is the only certainty they have. As the music continues to fade, however, Olga can only lament the blindness with which they must make their way through life, working without any proof of reward. Everything and nothing has changed, the past remains inaccessible, and the future is without promise. The action of the play is the raising of hopes and the crushing of them. The resolution is a coming to terms with reality, at least for one of the sisters—Olga.

In Caryl Churchill's *Far Away*, a young girl has come to live with her aunt and can't sleep because she has witnessed some horrors on the property. The young girl questions her aunt about seeing her uncle hitting people with an iron bar. The young girl, Joan, had climbed out of bed and into a tree in the yard, where she witnessed the uncle bundling someone into the shed, and then witnessed children in a shed with blood on their faces. The aunt at first denies it, says Joan saw things she shouldn't have, and then admits that one of the people the uncle was hitting was found to be a traitor, and that the whole family will now be on the side of right, fighting the traitors. "You're part of a big movement now to make things better," says the aunt to the child. So the first scene is one of a world we don't recognize, but we do, and it is one filled with violence and portends worse. When I saw the first scene I was reminded of China in the days preceding Tiananmen Square. There was something "bad" in the air.

By the end of the play, and several years later, the entire world is at war, chained prisoners march on their way to execution, Joan returns to her aunt's house, and describes her journey on the way.

JOAN

There were piles of bodies, and if you stopped to find out there was one killed by coffee, or one killed by pins, they were killed by heroin, petrol, chainsaws, hairspray, bleach, foxgloves, the smell of smoke was where we were burning the grass that wouldn't serve... There was a camp of Chilean soldiers upstream but they hadn't seen me and fourteen black and white cows downstream having a drink so I knew I'd have to go straight across. But I didn't know whose side the river was on, it might help me swim or it might drown me. In the middle the current was running much faster, the water was brown, I didn't know if that meant anything. I stood on the bank a long time. But I knew it was my only way of getting here so at last I put one foot in the river. It was very cold but so far that was all. When you've just stepped in you can't tell what's going to happen. The water laps round your ankles in any case.

There is an unsettling resemblance to the events in Paris in 2015. *Far Away* begins in a world beginning to go awry and ends with a world gone completely out of control, where there is little hope for respite. Only the most insignificant physical facts can be counted on.

James C. Nicola (artistic director of New York Theatre Workshop) said of *Far Away*, "I couldn't help but look at the play as a response to Caryl's dealing with her love of her grandchildren and thinking, 'What do I say to them about the horrific world that we live in, and how can I prepare them for it without intimidating them?'" Churchill is reminding us from the play's very start, in which someone is pushing someone into a shed, through the Parade of the Hats, led by a procession of ragged, beaten, and chained prisoners on their way to execution, that we are all dehumanized. Churchill leaves us with the image of devastation as witnessed by a young girl, and shows us the innocence and strength with which she faces adversity. At the start of the play, Joan is at her Aunt Harper's house and can't sleep. By the end of the play, Harper warns Joan, "You can't stay here, they'll be after you, they'll be after you," and Joan is trying to escape through the mountains, through "rats bleeding out of their mouths and ears," and past the dead bodies. It's not certain how far away she can get from this world.

Sam Shepard's *Curse of the Starving Class* tells the story of a family in rural California. No one in the family is physically starving, but they are hungry for identity and selfhood, for roots, for status and place. The journey of the play is a quest for self-esteem and a larger place in the universe. Nobody gets that, but one member of the family, Wesley, sees that his only choice is to give up the dream and cling to the roots he already has. The family is torn apart by the very thing that binds them together: their desire to escape their lower-middle-class lives. They want something better for themselves, but they don't know where that is or how to get there. There is an emptiness that they can't fill. This is symbolized onstage by their refrigerator, which they are continually opening, staring into, and finding nothing to their liking, slamming it shut. Ella says to Wesley, "How can you be hungry all the time? We're not poor. We're not rich but we're not poor." Wesley replies, "What are we then?" The action of the play is the family trying to find this out. Ella promises that they're going to have some money real soon, and then their lives will change. Their search is not unlike that of the Youngers in Lorraine Hansberry's *A Raisin in the Sun*, or Chekhov's three sisters.

In the course of the play, the father, Weston, is constantly borrowing money for things he can't afford: land in the desert, liquor, cars. His wife, Ella, threatens to sell their house and head for Europe. Their daughter, Emma, threatens to take the horse and run away to Mexico. Only the son, Wesley, has resisted the family's self-destruction. By the play's end, however, he too has lost hope, putting on his father's discarded, dirty clothes. By this point, Ella has passed out on the kitchen table, and Weston has presumably left home to avoid the bill collectors. Emma, the daughter, has taken the keys to her mother's car and is about to start a journey of her own. Ella wakes screaming just as her daughter is leaving. Suddenly, there is an explosion outside that rocks the house. The bill collectors, Emerson and Slater, have arrived. They enter, giggling, and when Wesley asks what blew up, they say, "Something that wasn't paid for. Something past due." They have blown up the car, and Emerson says, "Well, that's what comes from not paying your bills."

The final image of the play is of an eagle and a cat locked in a struggle that neither can win. This is the end of a story that Weston had begun earlier, in which he feeds lamb testicles to a soaring eagle. Ella and Wesley stand perfectly still, facing in opposite directions. Ella finishes the story, picking up where her husband left off.

ELLA

They fight like crazy in the middle of the sky. That cat's tearing his chest out, and the eagle's trying to drop him, but the cat won't let go because he knows if he falls he'll die.

WESLEY

And the eagle's being torn apart in midair. The eagle's trying to free himself from the cat, and the cat won't let go.

ELLA

And they come crashing down to the earth. Both of them come crashing down. Like one whole thing.

The image of this cursed family is echoed in the image of the eagle and the cat. They are in a struggle, which results in the absence of the father, the death of the daughter, and the mother and son are left, witnessing the devastation, part of the same cursed entity, but never really connecting.

We've looked at a variety of effective endings, but it's impossible to know the process by which their authors reached them. I would suggest reading playwrights' letters and biographies and trying to gain insight into their processes and intentions. I would particularly recommend *Playwrights at Work*, published by the Paris Review, and *Playwrights in Rehearsal*, published by Routledge. I can however, address some of my own plays, and the processes I used to forge my endings.

In my one-act play *The Bridge at Belharbour*, which takes place on the north shore of Boston, a suburban widow, Valerie Marino, emerges as something of an angel of death. She has called a plumber, Tom Fahey, to her house overlooking the Atlantic, to clear her stopped-up drain. There is an obvious class difference between the woman and the plumber, and she is anxious to mine that difference for all it's worth, assaulting the plumber's dignity. In the course of the one-hour play, played in real time, she manages to elicit enough information about the plumber to discover all his vulnerabilities. Every stated truth in the play is conditional and problematical, and shaped by forces crouching just out of view.

Midway through the play, Valerie flirts with Tom.

VALERIE

You've been watching me, haven't you, out of the corner of your eyes? Don't be afraid.

TOM

I ain't.

But shortly after, when Tom succumbs to her obvious gesture towards him, and goes to kiss her movie-star fashion (which is the best he can summon up) she pulls away in disgust. This is the beginning of the end for Tom. Valerie, from the beginning, has set out to destroy this stranger, out of a kind of misplaced retaliation for her own miseries.

TOM

What do you think I am? Some dumb slob you can cast off like a fly. You can't fool around with people like that. I shouldn't have done that... you made me.

VALERIE

I didn't make you do anything... Oh, go home, why don't you, home to your wife and your seven ugly kids and your above ground swimming pool and the big holes in your mouth where your teeth fell out and you haven't got the money to replace them. I saw. I saw when your mouth was open.

And this is only the beginning of the assault.

By the end of the play, Valerie has succeeded in crushing what small ego Tom has, and the conclusion suggests Tom's planned suicide on the way home. This suicide, off the bridge at Belharbour, echoes Valerie's reverie about the same bridge, and how some days it is just waiting for her, and how she would like to fly off of it, like some bird.

VALERIE

The leaves are blowing upside down.

TOM

Heat's gonna break.

VALERIE

It's started to rain. Maybe you ought to leave before the storm gets too bad.

TOM

Yeah, I'd better get moving.

VALERIE

Maybe you shouldn't take the shore road.

TOM

Yeah. I'm real tired.

VALERIE

Perhaps you ought to use the new highway instead.

TOM

By way of that bridge you was talkin' about before.

VALERIE

What bridge?

TOM

The one you said they built just for you.

VALERIE

For me?

TOM

You said...

VALERIE

You hear what you want to hear, Mr. Fahey.

TOM

No. You said the bridge at Belharbour is waiting...

(VALERIE shrugs her shoulders)

Well guess I'd better be going. Sorry I never got the sink unplugged.

VALERIE

I'll find someone else.

(And then leaving the opals he had bought for his wife as a birthday present, and which Valerie had pronounced to be bad luck)

VALERIE

Don't forget the opals.

TOM

Keep 'em. I don't want them.

VALERIE

You sure?

TOM

I'm sure... well so long... and good luck to you.

VALERIE

I already used up my good luck.

TOM

Nah, I don't think so. Goodbye Mrs Marino.

(TOM exits)

VALERIE

I'm sorry, but everyone has to live. It's such a crowded planet.

At this point, with Tom gone, she chillingly takes out the package with the opals in it, unwraps it, and puts on the opal necklace. Valerie is an even match for Hedda Gabler. What I always liked about the ending of *The Bridge at Belharbour* is the spareness of language that echoes the silence of death. It's in the sounds and the rhythms. All I can remember of the writing of it is the utter quietude and slow, steady march to the end. At that moment all the reins were in my hands.

In writing the end of a recent play, *After Marseilles*, I began by rereading what I had written so far, and then reviewed all the notes I had made on the play, culled from a reading at the O'Neill, one at Primary Stages in New York, from colleagues and audiences for the readings, and my own comments and clarifications.

After Marseilles was begun on the eve of the millennium. Looking back at history, it seemed to me more and more marked by random acts of violence, and then, less randomly, greed, ambition, and the erosion of the environment and public trust. We were becoming a world without a moral backbone. Our focus had been accumulation and power, and we seemed like a runaway train, heading for disaster.

"What if," I thought, "we were forced to live with a disaster of our own making, or, because of natural forces or a combination; how would we recreate a new world?"

The play opens in a world that has been destroyed by a natural catastrophe. It is the end of civilization as we know it. Five characters—Sam, Dakota, Zoe, Chip, and Madame Zaza—are blown onto the rocky coast of Marseilles, much the same as Odysseus was driven onto the coast of a strange land. In the face of government intimidation, and led by Madame Zaza, a native of Paris and a clothes designer, they try to rebuild.

Because we write to find out what it is we are writing about, it is not until three quarters of the way through and usually the second draft, at least, that we begin to understand the full complexity of what we're working on and the questions it's asking. In addition, if we have done our homework and conceived biographies for all the characters and worked out the backstory, encompassing that time the characters spent before they all walked into your play, some of the characters will start to take us in a direction we couldn't have possibly imagined in any outline. You have to trust that. If you listen to your characters they will tell you what their deepest desires are, and you will understand what they are trying to get in the play and what is standing in their way.

The following are some excerpts from the hundreds of pages of notes I made while writing the first four drafts of *After Marseilles*.

They are the major comments I used in order to write the end of the play to my satisfaction. Since Madame Zaza is the major character, it was her journey I was concentrating on, looking for hints in my notes and in her lines in the play.

"Zaza is doing everything she does in order to prevent herself from dying... dealing with the waning of her life."

"What are Zaza's honest emotions at every moment in the play?"

"Zaza realizes in the end she is doomed to mortality."

"To stop death in its tracks one has to look for meaning in the present."

"Tragedy shows us the best and worst of human beings."

"How to have the courage of your own life in an age without morality or reason."

"Is there reason in an unreasonable universe?"

"Let Zaza reveal herself through an action"

"On the Day of Atonement it is written in The Book, who shall die and who shall live that year. Zaza sees her name written in the book."

"There is a longing to go back to America. Many Americans thought they wanted a European kind of sophistication, but now want community and their own roots."

"Make everyone's yearnings real so their disappointments can be real."

"As long as the other characters stay, Zaza has a purpose."

"How do we get from destruction to possibility?"

"This has been the bloodiest century in the history of the human race." (From an editorial in the *New York Times* by James Reston, May 30, 1982.)

"A small act of love redeems the characters."

"In the blues the human spirit is acknowledging both pain and soaring."

"Is Zaza a fool or a prophet?"

"What pushes the play forward is Zaza's desire to live, to continue in the face of hopelessness."

"I think of the future as stretching before me and I go forward to meet it."

"Man takes a positive hand whenever he puts a building in the earth beneath the sun."

"To overcome our feelings of hopelessness and channel our rage and anguish towards constructive ends." (From an editorial in the *New York Times*, October 2002, entitled "Betraying Humanity," by Bob Herbert.)

"Stakes is what a character has to win or lose."

"What is it that shatters Zaza's spirit? When she is found out to be lying? When she realizes she has to let everyone go and face her own death alone?"

"What does Zaza want? To hold onto her life spirit and to never give up. To be in control."

"What I love about Zaza—she has the courage of her own life. She is a celebrant. She does not want to leave life, and so her reluctance to let it all go... but she can not keep back the tides."

At one moment, when I was nearing the end of one of my drafts of the play, I had a strong feeling that Zaza was trying to hold back the ocean from rolling on, to stop the inevitable tides. It was this strong pull and image that ultimately gave me the end of my play and contributed to the note, above, about holding back the ocean.

This moment with *After Marseilles* and Zaza was the one in which I truly discovered that we write to learn what it is we are writing about. The play was originally conceived from a *New York Times* article about this century being the bloodiest in history. That editorial was from 1982, but it was not until the year 2000 that I would revisit the article and start the play. I had recently visited Marseilles and found it to be a kind of crossroads of the world. It occurred to me that if the world ever ended, this is where it would end, at the tip of France, where Europe connects to Africa. And I was off!

I know, as a teacher of dramatic writers, an outline should ideally be demanded at the start; but, to be honest, I have never followed a complete outline, for the very reason stated above—that we write to find out our subject. In addition, the character work, if it is done in depth, takes over at some point, and the characters lead us out of their desires. I often ask for an outline, but I know it will never be completely followed. It is meant as a blueprint to get started and to see where you think you are going.

That image of Zaza trying to hold back the ocean is one of those epiphany moments that are the absolute joy of being a writer. Our work is to solve problems, and here the answer was on a golden platter. I understood the metaphor perfectly. Zaza wanted to hold onto life, to hold back her own mortality. And it came out of her very love of life. I did recognize my own feelings, subconscious as they were. I was on the other side of fifty now, and didn't know exactly how I'd gotten there, but wanted this aging to stop! If only I could hold back the tides. That was Zaza's secret and she held it from me until the second draft. It came to me at the O'Neill Playwrights Center, sitting at my desk, looking out onto the Atlantic, waves rolling in and back.

Here are the last pages of *After Marseilles*.

DAKOTA

A gale's blowing in. Us fishermen love weather.

(SAM enters carrying two pieces of luggage)

SAM

They found it! They found your luggage. It arrived this morning,

(The sounds of a bird, low pitched, grating, loud, insistent, like wagon wheels across bricks)

ZOE

What's that?

SAM

Fork-tailed drongo. It has a low, mournful sound, like "whoo whee" ... listen.

(Repeated sound of bird)

It warns all the other animals that danger's near. It smells it before it appears. In the bush, to the south, it warns the smaller animals of predators, of leopards or lions. That's his sound. I know it.

(ZAZA gets up from the table, returns to the shop she's building, hammering up more boards. The bird continues to call. The sky becomes darker)

SAM

Something's coming over the bridge, from the south, with the storm. Far away, but you can hear... packs of hyenas, lions, herds of elephants, buffalo, and rhino.

DAKOTA

How do you know?

(During the following exchange it starts to rain, light at first, then harder)

SAM

My grandmother taught me birds and animals; she taught me to listen. She believed all animals were sacred. The drongo is warning the littlest ones, the young cubs, the impalas, that a leopard is coming, walking alone. The leopards are the holiest and the fiercest, and always unaccompanied. They're likely coming from the Kruger, or from the Serengeti, even as far as the Cape of Good Hope. I can never be sure what I'm hearing, but I feel it. We should leave. It's time to go.

CHIP

To where?

ZAZA

You could try west, on foot, up through the Pyrenees, or north through the Alps. Go.

DAKOTA

Then come on. Let's get going, Zaza.

ZAZA

I'm not coming.

DAKOTA

What do you mean? Oh yes you are.

                    ZAZA

No. I need to finish building my shop. My heart's set on it.

(They all just stand there)

Go ahead! Go! Get out of here! And don't feel badly for me. I lived the life I wanted.

(They all remain standing. The rain continues. Sound of animals is nearer)

Move. Go! One, two, three, one, two, three... You too, Sam.

(They start leaving, but in the opposite direction of the bridge that supposedly connects to Africa. They leave behind the found luggage. Then they stop, hesitate, look back for a moment at ZAZA)

                    ZAZA

In Spain, you know, there are oranges on the trees.

                SAM (to ZAZA)

Let us know you got home safely.

                    ZAZA

I will. And who knows? After Marseilles? Maybe there's something better... or something.

(They EXIT, disappearing, as if into light, leaving ZAZA alone on the stage, hammering away at her new shop. The rain stops. The wind dies down. Sound of the bird)

In rereading the end of the play, it is interesting that both *The Bridge at Belharbour*, an early piece, and *After Marseilles*, a much later one, both end with weather. And yet I cannot think of another dramatic piece I've written that ends with weather. There is, however, a shared element in the endings: they reflect a probable death for one of the characters. I think it is simulated in the rhythm of the rising storm and the subsequent silence at the very close. In many ways it is similar to the hush of the falling snow at the end of the film *Coming Home*.

The last scene of *After Marseilles*, called "Le Banquet Finale," takes place at a celebratory banquet, heralding the end of a long famine, except that all the food has been stolen—crab cakes and raspberry tarts. To understand the ending and the characters and themes it is pulling together, it is necessary to know Zoe and Chip had lost their luggage at the beginning of the play, and have been waiting for it to be located. Madame Zaza, prior to the banquet, has been building a dress shop to replace the elegant one she once owned in Paris. As part of the set, there is also a bridge that is rumored to go to Africa. Other than Madame Zaza, the other four are from the US, or what used to be the US, and there is hardly a chance they are ever going to make it anywhere, once they decide to leave. But they are going to try. It also comes as quite a surprise that Madame Zaza is not going with them. At the end, they reluctantly leave her behind, and it all makes sense.

So how did I come to these choices? Well, first, the image of animals coming two by two, from Africa, and over the bridge, came to me. The imagery, obviously, is from the flood in the Bible, signaling terrible times coming. But these animals, rather than entering the safety of an ark, are raging wildly, and together with the mournful call of the bird constitute an ominous force.

Once the image came to me, it was clear Zaza would choose to stay, ready now to face the very mortality she has been trying to hold back. Also, she would finally let go of the others, realizing she has to be alone in order to let go, and in this case, to die. I then remembered a close friend who had suffered a long illness, saying, at the last, not to feel pity for her as she had lived the very life she wanted. That was a gift to give a friend, and a line that always had, for me, resonant clarity and dignity and grace. I loved being able to use it for Zaza, because in the course of the play she comes to a similar recognition and owns her biography.

In addition, I remembered a guide from a visit to Africa, who once told me all the signs and sounds his grandfather had taught him. I was amazed he was the only one in this particular part of Africa who knew how to find a leopard alone in the wild, just by the direction birds were flying and other animals leaving. Every animal, he told me, left the path clear for the leopard, both because of his ferociousness and out of respect for him as one of the royal members of the animal kingdom. I also chose to have Zaza building for a future she could not expect, but only hope for—the same as the others who would be traveling in the opposite direction to Africa, through the Pyrenees. In an earlier section of the play, it is reported the Mediterranean is full of dead bodies and not navigable. I can not tell you where the line "In Spain, you know, there are oranges on the trees" came from, except that I would not want to say directly that they would be going through

Spain, so this is a way of saying it, and again, articulating it with hope, in the image of oranges growing on trees. When Sam tells Zaza to let them know when she gets home safely, he is, of course, referring to some kind of afterlife.

The very last line of the play came long after I had decided on a title. I meant the title to refer to the question of what could possibly be expected after any catastrophe, and especially the one that exists at the top of the play. The last line just came out of Zaza's mouth. She wrote it. She was, after all, looking for something better. How could the writer have possibly known this in the beginning? By the time you come to the end, you know the characters so well and their journey, they are truly, like all good characters, writing the very lines for you.

How do you know you are at the end? In some ways you never do. The scene that completes the project may only come in rehearsal or production. Just make certain you end your project authoritatively, when the conflicts are resolved. Be disciplined. Don't try to write the entire world in your ending. Your story only has one ending—the one you choose to complete your story.

This is some of what I know about writing an ending.

> Lecture delivered to a group of Advanced Playwriting
> students, Tisch School of the Arts, Goldberg Department
> of Dramatic Writing, Fall 2004

Exercises

1 Look at the endings of Tennessee Williams' *The Glass Menagerie*, Paula Vogel's *How I Learned To Drive*, and Polly Stenham's *That Face*. Then go back and trace the themes in the three plays, analyzing how the authors came to those endings and what those endings accomplish.

2 For the same three plays, what three different endings could you construct and how would that change the meaning of the plays?

3 Write a poem based on something you feel passionate about. Then take the last line and write it as a last scene in a screenplay or play, fashioning the backstory based on the rest of your poem. Is it possible you may have the idea for a new dramatic piece here?

Assignment

Complete rewriting the second half of your script, referring to Chapter 9 on rewriting.
  Identify the focus (spine) and theme for your piece.*
  Make certain you have nailed it.
  Paste the focus and theme near your computer, so you are constantly reminded to keep on track.

---

* As you write and rewrite, the focus and theme may become clearer and you can change them as this occurs.

Week 8
Checkpoints

Reviewing your project
Common errors
The most effective writing

This is an opportunity to pause and ask a series of questions.

The following checkpoints are formulated to help you in going forward while you are still *in process*. It is a safeguard to ensure that you're on the right path with your script. It is also meant as a guide to your rewriting (Chapter 9).

1. Make certain you are telling a fascinating story. Do you get passionate when relating the story? If not, listen to that. The author has to love the project as much as a parent loves a child.
2. What did your major character want? Did they get it? Did they get something else? How does the chasing after the dream affect the action of the piece? Who is the most complex character in the script and why?
3. What were the major obstacles for the character getting what they wanted? Make certain something is obstructing and challenging them.
4. Which character has not had a scene yet in the script? What is the benefit to the story of presenting this character later in the script or series of episodes? Would there be an advantage to the character entering earlier?
5. What secret has been revealed so far?
6. Find one scene you could eliminate from the script. Find one speech you could eliminate. Which is your strongest scene and why?
7. Is there clarity? Does the audience know what this series or play or screenplay is about? Do you? Can you state it in one sentence?
8. What is the biggest surprise in your narrative?
9. The audience is always waiting to see what happens. What answer are they waiting to discover?

10 Does the action keep moving? Remember that too much description or "talk" keeps the story from advancing at a good pace. You cannot be self-indulgent. Recently, a student began a screenplay including long passages from a novel. He acknowledged they were there because they "stated" the theme. When he was told they were holding back the story and either should be cut or trimmed, he nodded his head, but in a rewrite never cut them. The script didn't take off until page three, and that is too late.
11 If it is a linear story, how does one action lead to the next? Is there a chain of events?
12 If it is a non-linear story, do all the pieces add up to a focused core? Is there a cumulative chain of events?
13 Can you identify the turning points in your story?
14 Where is the script daring? When your writing takes chances it has unexpected incidents, distant from the "norm," or something never seen before. A new way of telling a story.

After sitting on dozens of panels choosing dramatic-writing grants or production recipients, the following is a list of the common mistakes, or the major reasons projects often get turned down, followed by a list of common characteristics of the winners.

Common errors

1 Excessive verbiage. Overwriting.
2 Lack of originality and predictability.
3 Lack of clarity. What is the dramatic piece about?
4 Dreadful dialogue. Trite, flat, banal, generic, and not particular to each character. Inconsistency in the speech of characters.
5 Lack of complexity.
6 Lack of conflict and dramatic incident.
7 Underdeveloped characters, one-note characterizations
8 Underwriting—not exploring all the possible explosive moments.
9 Lack of focus. Overstuffing your bag so there is a little bit of everything in it.
10 Turning in an early draft. Failure to edit and rewrite.

Successful dramatic projects have the following characteristics in common

1 Originality. A fresh idea no one has ever heard before.
2 Selectivity. There is no "fat" in the script.

3   Superb dialogue. All the characters have individual and identifiable voices.
4   Clear focus and theme. The audience and you know exactly what this is about.
5   We can identify with one or more of the characters and therefore empathize.
6   A mesmerizing story. The audience is keenly interested in finding out what happens. The story pulls you in. The author is clearly invested.
7   The reader or audience is moved.
8   Theatricality. The script may be successfully staged or shot.
9   Relevant contemporary subject matter or historical material.
10 Your piece has a beginning, middle, and end. The beginning should be rapid, setting out the problem; the middle should build in excitement and complications; the end should complete the script's promise.

Exercises

Correct any of the common errors listed if they are present in your script.

Check all positive checkpoint elements, making sure they are in your script. If not, how can you include them?

Assignment

Complete the first draft of your script, incorporating any changes stimulated by this chapter on checkpoints.

Week 9
Rewriting

The writer Bernard Malamud says he would write a project at least three times—"once to understand it, the second time to improve it, and a third to compel it to say what it must say."

It's difficult to accept we are only beginning our journey with a dramatic piece when we finish the first draft. In order to face the series of rewrites it needs and deserves, it is best to approach the task in a formulaic way, so you have an orderly set of steps to follow and don't feel overwhelmed. In rewriting, first make a list of problems you need to tackle, and attack one problem at a time, then cross it off. For example, if you have to deepen one character's voice, work on that throughout the script, from beginning to end. Then, if you have some plot problems, reshuffle the plot so that it all flows together. Don't attack all your problems at the same time. List them, and vanquish them like dragons, one at a time.

Common problems to solve/things to do in a rewrite (and some suggestions)

Strengthen a character's voice

Suggestion: if you haven't yet found your character's voice (and you will know because all that character's speeches are generic rather than individualized), then ask your character a central question about their childhood or their mother, and have them answer in their own voice. You will find the character's voice this way, providing you write it honestly, and from the character's point of view—not that of you, the writer.

Deepen characterization

Suggestion: if you find one of your characters lacks complexity, look up the word "complex" in the dictionary. The Oxford English Dictionary defines it as "Integrated, or something that is not easily analyzed or disentangled." A complex character should have many opposing parts in their personality that encompasses both their Apollonian and Dionysian aspects.

In order to create a more complex character, ask your character a question that involves their ethical standards. Have them answer in their own voice.

"It is the week before Christmas and you are frantic. You have a huge paper due the next day, plus you are buying presents, throwing a party, and trying to deal with an unusual skin rash that has erupted. Your brother wants to borrow money because his new band isn't getting gigs, and he has no cash for presents. Your parents demand you come home for a week over the holidays because they miss you, and also, they paid your college tuition. In the middle of this, a friend calls, saying they are desperately lonely, and could you meet them tonight and just go to a movie? What do you do? What do you tell your parents? What do you tell your brother? What do you tell your professors?"

The answers will tell you a lot about your characters because characters are defined by their choices.

I like to put characters in a tight spot and test them, because I know people who are pleasant but not accommodating; accommodating but full of anger; fun but self-centered; morose but witty and kind. We are all a network of complex characteristics, based on genetics, our upbringings, social interactions and pressures, and our experiences.

The plot is not complex enough and lacks a large enough conflict to lead to a dramatic incident

Suggestion: read the Bible, the storylines of operas, or the daily newspaper or weekly news magazine in order to get ideas about plot complications. The bottom line is this: the complications of a plot are based on what the central character wants and just how far they will go to get it. So, go back and ask that question of your protagonist: "What do you really want? How far are you willing to go to get it?"

Editing

Your script is hugely overwritten. How do you know? First, your pages are dense with language and have very little "air." Second, there are interchanges that, though pleasant and real, do not further plot or characterization.

Suggestions: go through every single phrase, line, and speech, and see what you can lose. If something is neither the result of previous action, or the cause of future action, it's unnecessary.

If you start to feel your script is mainly conversational, or marking time and not moving forward, see where you can make a large cut while maintaining the sense of the piece. In any rewrite, you must be able to let go of writing you are enamored with. If you have a good line, you can always write it on a postcard.

So, go through every long speech and see if it is intrinsic to the script, or if it is you, the writer, speaking. Next, see how many sentences and phrases you can lose from within the speech to make it shorter and sharper. Cut the fat.

When you've completed your first round of editing, go back to the beginning and do it again. This editing process will continue through possible rehearsals, depending on the kind of project and the director, until the script is as tight as you can make it. I have never reread a script, or been in a reading, workshop, or rehearsal for a full production of a play where I did not cut lines and it made the piece better.

Sometimes, instead of writing too much, we underwrite

Emotional moments are ignored or a large recognition and reversal is completed in one or two lines. Often, we need many steps going towards the moment of climax. Since it isn't mathematical, no one can tell you how many; it is more like a piece of music or a poem, in that you will know when it is just right.

Suggestion: improvise the moment with an actor and you'll often get your answer. I use this method in class when a writer has failed to realize the depth of a passionate moment. We improvise right on the spot, often between two or three sets of people, until we find it.

Individuation of voices

Sometimes we get two characters speaking in the same voice. This is simply a matter of redoing your biographical homework.

Suggestion: first, decide which character the doubled voice will belong to. Then draw up a new set of biographical questions to ask the other character, interviewing them, asking leading questions, and redoing every speech belonging to that character. It's important to take on the physical and emotional complexities of your character during every speech so that they are reacting anew. Be warned this may change the plot, but it will certainly make for a more honest dramatic piece.

Lack of clarity

No one understands what your play is about, or they understand too late.

Suggestion: go back to the major conflict of the piece. Ask yourself why you wanted to write this piece and what it is basically about. Now that you're sure of your focus, go back and make certain the audience knows what the main problem is in the first five minutes. If they don't, you will lose them. Often the writer is clear on the subject of his project, but fails to communicate it quickly enough, choosing subtlety over clarity. If the protagonist plans to bake the biggest bagel in Chicago (as my teacher Israel Horovitz once suggested), find this out in the opening minutes of the piece. In Marsha Norman's play *'Night, Mother* we know from the beginning that Jessie wants to kill herself. She tells her mother so. The secret of the play's tension is that the audience spends the evening waiting to see whether or not she'll actually do it.

Order of scenes

In a linear play, one scene should push the next scene forward. In a non-linear play, you have a constellation of scenes, which should connect thematically. Either way, there should be a forward motion. If you do not have this momentum, you need to reorder or even eliminate a scene.

Suggestion: list the action of each scene on separate index cards. Also, give each scene a title, such as "The Humiliation Scene," "The Scene of Huge Disappointment," "Discovery of the Secret," or "Joyful Connection." Place all these index cards on your desk or floor in the order that they now appear in the play. Do they form an increasing set of conflicts that lead to a confrontation? What is the build of emotion for each character? How could you reorder the scenes to make the piece more dramatic?

The ending is not satisfying

Suggestion: please refer to Chapter 8 on endings. Ernest Hemingway wrote the last page of *A Farewell to Arms* forty-four times before he finally got it right.

Do your rewrite methodically

Remember: deal with one problem at a time. Cross each rewriting problem off your list as you go, making certain all your revisions are organic to the completed script.

Barbara Greenberg, a Boston poet, short-fiction writer, and co-author of the children's musical *Jeremy and the Thinking Machine*, as well as a teacher of creative writing, gave the following advice:

> To rewrite: first, edit out whatever seems inauthentic, derivative, and/or lazy. In the process of editing, re-engage with what was valid and original in the former draft. Then, with luck, rewrite from that source. Language and technique will often rise to the challenge.

Ernest Hemingway would go back over his work every day from the beginning, and rewrite. This was critical to his process. As several chapters began to develop, he'd go back two or three chapters in order to continue the piece with the proper "tone." Early drafts of his writing are very undisciplined, rambling all over the place, and include many false starts. Hemingway's lean, disciplined style made the writing seem simple. He focused on one point and wrote very clearly about that. But if we put the stories together, a complex picture emerges. "There's no rule on how it is to write," Hemingway wrote his editor Charles Poore in 1953. "Sometimes it comes easily and perfectly. Sometimes it is like drilling rock and then blasting it out with charges." Because *A Farewell to Arms* was being serialized in *Scribner's Magazine*, Hemingway had six months to struggle with the ending. He left forty-four pages of alternate endings, a record even for the meticulous Hemingway, who would write out or retype a page until he was satisfied with it. Fitzgerald sent Hemingway ten handwritten pages of comments on the draft of the novel, and Hemingway's response was "Kiss my ass" (www.vergemag.com/0201/features/feat2.html from http://www.jfklibrary.org/eh.htm).

August Wilson, in reference to *Jitney*, his 1970s play, which premiered in Pittsburgh in 1982, re-premiered at the Pittsburgh Public in 1996, and opened at Boston's Huntington Theatre prior to a Broadway revival in 2000, said:

> Marion McClinton is directing and we're going to scrap everything else, the set and the costumes. We may use some of the same actors, but we're going to start over and I'm going to do some re-writes, particularly the Becker-Booster scenes" - the father and

son. "I want to rethink the whole character of Booster. I wrote that 18, 19 years ago now, and I think maybe if I reimagine it, now that I'm more mature, they'll *say different things*.
(www.post-gazette.com/magazine/19980324bwilson5.asp).

In the Spring 2001 issue of *African American Review*, Elisabeth J. Heard writes about *Jitney*:

> The revision of Jitney sparked an interest among critics in Wilson's revision strategies. Critic Herrington states, "The changes Wilson made to Jitney reflected a new methodology of playwriting—specifically of rewriting—which he had developed while working on *Seven Guitars* at the Goodman Theatre in Chicago in 1995." This "new methodology" involved not rewriting the play before the rehearsal. Instead, Wilson waited until the rehearsal process began and then made daily changes to the script. If he felt that a scene needed to be changed or that a monologue should be added, Wilson would go home, do the rewrite, and bring the changes to rehearsal the next day. I asked Wilson about this revision strategy.

> HEARD: I read that you experimented with a new revision strategy for this play. Will you continue to use this strategy with future plays?
> WILSON: You are talking about writing in the moment?
> HEARD: Yes, getting feedback from the actors and directors, writing new parts, and bringing them the next day.
> WILSON: That's a good way to work. I don't know if it is necessarily a new way to work because generally I'd do the whole rewrite, come to rehearsal, and continue to work on it. But one time when I did *Seven Guitars*, I did the rewrite during the rehearsal process, and it seemed to work as well if not better than the other way. I guess I'm not consciously aware that I made a change, but I'll certainly continue doing what I'm doing, working the way I'm working, and enjoy the rehearsal process and working through there. So I will continue that.
> In the past I would rewrite the whole thing and bring it in, and, of course, there were certain revisions that were made in the rehearsal process. But the bulk of the work had been done, so I would sort of lay back off of it (if that's a way of saying it) because I already did the rewrite, and now I was just patching up

various things. With *Seven Guitars* I didn't do the rewrite prior to rehearsal. I came into rehearsal knowing that the play had to be rewritten. And I did my rewrite there in rehearsal, which didn't allow me to lay back off the material and do patchwork. I had to get in there and do the actual work, which seemed to work better in the sense that I wasn't writing in a vacuum. I had the actors there, so you could press and then you could see a response, or you could do something and see an immediate response. If you're at home doing the rewrite, you can't get that response – you're sort of working in a vacuum, so to speak.

HEARD: Were there other benefits from writing in the moment and getting the immediate feedback?

WILSON: I think so. it is a different kind of work, so you write different things. I think that if I'm at home sitting doing the rewrite, I'm going to write something different than if I'm there in the rehearsal room doing it. It's kind of hard to explain, but if you're tossed into the fire at any particular moment, then you are going to write something different than you will in another particular moment. And that is from day to day. Here at this moment on Tuesday at this rehearsal I'll come up with this, and I'm going to rewrite that; I'm going to rewrite it tonight. If I rewrite it next week I'm going to write something different. So you have to choose what is the right moment to do it because you sort of only get to do it once. I found more immediacy in the rehearsal process. I certainly wrote different things—I don't know if I wrote better things—and I enjoyed it.

Chekhov maintained in regards to rewriting:

> I shall finish my story to-morrow or the day after, but not to-day, for it has exhausted me fiendishly towards the end. Thanks to the haste with which I have worked at it, I have wasted a pound of nerves over it. The composition of it is a little complicated. I got into difficulties and often tore up what I had written, and for days at a time was dissatisfied with my work—that is why I have not finished it till now. How awful it is! I must rewrite it! It's impossible to leave it, for it is in a devil of a mess. My God! If the public likes my works as little as I do those of other people, which I am reading, what an ass I am! There is something asinine about our writing.
> (Chekhov's letters, August 6, 1891)

Tina Howe, New York playwright and professor of Writing for Theatre at Hunter College in New York, had the following to say about the process of rewriting:

> Writing a play is an exercise in stamina, blind faith and insanity. More than anything it calls for compression. Getting down on your hands and knees and beating things down to their essence. It's loud and messy work. You scream, weep and tear out your hair in fistfuls. After years of doing this, I've finally come up with an image that encapsulates the whole gruesome process.
>
> An idea for a new play is like an enormous lake – something really huge like Lake Erie, but instead of being filled with water, it's filled with rubber cement – shimmering, viscous and smelly. As your ideas start to sharpen, the lake miraculously starts to shrink. From a lake to a swimming hole and finally to a pond that you can circumnavigate in an afternoon. As your characters become more vivid, you find yourself kicking the outer edges of this pond until you can actually lean over and scoop it up in your arms. Handle it! Lick and poke it! Place it over your heart! When that happens it means the play is going to work! You're going to write it! And it's going to be your best ever!
>
> Then the real compression begins. Slapping and kneading the gooey mess until you can hold it in one hand. As the play takes shape, the script goes from the size of one of those huge plastic balls physical therapists use, to a medicine ball—to a basketball—to a volley ball—to a croquet ball—to a softball—to a baseball—to a ping pong ball—to a golf ball—to a marble and finally to a BB. As it compresses it gets harder, of course. When it reaches the golf ball stage it's as dense and heavy as a chunk of uranium. It you threw it out the window into the street, it would level an entire neighborhood.
>
> When, after two years of this relentless compression, it's finally the size of a BB, you have to proceed with caution as you roll it between your thumb and forefinger. It is rubber cement after all and it could just disappear into thin air. It's happened to me. I've polished and refined plays into grains of sand simply blew away. It's at this stage that you have to crawl out of your study, place it in a tiny box and give it to someone else to read.
>
> The entire process reverses itself once the play is accepted by a theater. You hand the company your gleaming BB, copies are made

until all the actors have one and then the ritual of release begins. As they knead their BBs, they get softer and softer. And bigger and bigger. Soon the floor is shimmering with rubber cement. It shudders and pools. As they bring the play to life, tides start to rise and suddenly we're back to our original lake. It's no longer my play! It belongs to all of us, and it's as vast and beautiful as any ocean you've ever seen.

For me, the process of rewriting *After Marseilles* took five years, although not contiguously, including six rewrites, and still counting. Since you have some background already on that play, the following are the notes I made and the questions I asked before starting each rewrite.

Rewrite 1

- How does the first monologue on "Blue" feed into the focus of the play?
- Read book entitled *Blue* and visit museum looking at paintings that utilize primarily the color blue, from the Renaissance through contemporary work. What may be the significance?
- Make certain all the wants of the characters are real so their disappointments are real.
- Is this a play about a yearning for an old America, and about the beliefs that we can always reinvent ourselves and transform?
- Madame Zaza's entrance should be much earlier.
- What does Madame Zaza want? Is she telling the truth?
- The last two scenes are right. How do I get there? It's where I want to go but the destination isn't yet earned.
- Do not lose the absurd for the mundane.
- What is Madame Zaza's reason for intervention?
- Why do people allow themselves to be bullied and not stand up? Are they afraid to trust their own feelings?

Rewrite 2

- Make sure the constant changing of the colored flags is dangerous enough.
- What are their honest emotions? Don't cerebrate.
- Chip is not developed enough as a mythic figure.
- Longing for community. Feel it!

- Is there a scene where they are all freed of authority and act like children?
- Are they destined to repeat their mistakes, or is that a red herring and not what the play is about at all?
- What is the major action of the play? If it is to get out of Marseilles, I don't believe it—but somewhere, the focus of the play is tied to that but I don't know how yet.
- Make it clear that Zoey is a journalist. Establish others identities—Madame Zaza as fashion designer, Chip as artist, Dakota as fisherwoman from Alaska, Sam as jazz musician.
- We have to believe that Zoe and Chip are in love.
- What is it that could break Zaza's spirit?
- Break down action of every scene in the play.
- What are the rising action and the climax? The climax has to do with something Madame Zaza, the protagonist, does.

Rewrite 3

- They all must be desperate and at each other's throats.
- What does Zaza want? To hold onto her life spirit? To never give up? To be in control? Then what could make her lose control? Remember that Zaza hates uncertainty.
- They must be terrified of being punished if they don't follow the government's rules. The danger has to be very real.
- The desire to rebuild physically is the right instinct.
- I know the end is destruction—but how? And what comes out of it?
- What does Sam really see on the other side of the bridge?
- Zaza has a secret. I don't know what it is yet. She's keeping it from even me, the author. I'll find out.
- At the end of the play do Zoe and Chip find their luggage and leave it on the stage? It's useless. The very thing they had sought is useless, without meaning.
- At least Zaza has the courage of her own life in an age without morality or reason. Zaza is the key to this play.
- Is someone saved by an act of grace like some character in a Carson McCullers story?
- Stakes is what the character has to win or lose—remember!
- Conflict is what prevents the character from getting what they want.

Rewrite 4

- Zaza has been lying about the government in Paris. There is no government. She did it to keep order and prevent chaos.
- How is she discovered? What is the moment? Who discovers it? Why did she do it?
- When does everyone find out? They must be furious at being betrayed.
- I keep hearing Madame Zaza saying she is trying to hold back the ocean. Isn't this trying to prevent time from moving on? Maybe she is trying to stave off her own death, like "Appointment in Samara." In the end she gives up? Why? Her spirit breaks down. Why? Could it be because she has been found out? Do the others forgive her? Forgiveness is gained if someone explains himself or herself. Perhaps if she apologizes and we believe her—that by keeping them all there, she can prevent her own death. You have die by yourself, alone. Maybe Zaza figures as long as she can keep everyone in Marseilles, even for false reasons, she can hold off her own aging and death.
- Part of living is the ability finally to let go.
- Picture of Zaza alone on stage at the end.

Rewrite 5

- Go through entire script and edit mercilessly. Get rid of at least 20 pages.
- Ultimately the people that inhabit this earth are going to have to figure out a way to forge a workable agreement on how to treat one another.
- Remember that each character is out to save their own skin.
- When they find out Zaza has been lying, not enough happens.
- Sam must be furious with himself for believing Zaza and going along with her. But the others must blame Sam by association. Sam also has to be angry with Zaza for making him her stooge. He should confront her.
- Each person has been betraying someone else in the story. How?
- Look at places where the characters are ruminative or meditative. Do they slow down the play? No lyrical outbursts, please!
- Make danger real if all do not obey, in the first scenes.
- We must care about Sam and know what he wants.
- Compassion for Zaza at the end of the play.

104 *Rewriting*

- We hear the animals coming over the bridge from Africa, at the end, and it signals a huge natural disaster that is the end of the play. Animals have the capacity to hear what humans can't. Knowing disaster is coming and the animals are running away from it, they all want Zaza to come away with them, through the Alps and Spain. Zaza refuses and asks them to leave her in peace alone.
- Last image is Zaza with her back to us, hammering away at the new dress shop she is building. We know it is useless, but she keeps on.

Rewrite 6

- We are free to behave the way we want, but we are responsible for our actions.
- What distinguishes us as humans is our empathy. Evil is the absence of compassion.
- They must discover how to behave when the shibboleth of the government is revealed and there are no rules.
- In the blues the human spirit is soaring. Go back to the original impetus of the play—the color blue.
- Zaza stops death in its tracks. The real search is for meaning. See Victor Frankl's book *Man's Search for Meaning*. Also reread J. Bronowski's *The Identity of Man*.
- Zaza knows in the end (realizes) that she is doomed to mortality. She had her turn.
- In a sense it is a dream play. Set in at beginning with lighting.
- One act of love redeems. All the others forgive Zaza and want her to escape with them, and that knowledge allows her to let go of them—the knowledge that she is wanted/loved.

The play began with a monologue about "Blueness" and I cannot tell you why. I do know I constructed the world of the play as one following a series of large natural disasters and man-made disasters, because of the escalating violence prevalent in the later part of the twentieth century. The opening image of the lost luggage in the play was based on a real incident, when I did once actually lose some luggage in Marseilles; and that feeling of Marseilles being both the end of the world and the actual crossroads of the world stayed with me. It is also of interest to note that in the last days of 2004, computerization broke down when thousands were flying, at Christmas time, and there were photos of acres of pieces of lost and abandoned luggage at airports. Was the play prescient? I don't think so. Rather, there are ideas floating in the air, at certain times in history, and disasters waiting to happen.

In the process of writing the play, and several workshops, its focus changed vastly. The process of rewriting this play was a prime example of writing to find out what it is you are writing about. I had to go through four drafts before the discovery that Zaza was trying to hold off her own mortality. When that moment came, the character herself whispered it to me and it was a shocking revelation. I remember thinking, "So this is what this whole play was about after all." It was thrilling. Once that discovery was made, it was easier to put the entire play into focus.

One of the more curious parts of the revision process was the end of the play. The idea of animals running from Africa, predicting some kind of large natural disaster, came to me in Rewrite 5. It was based on a guide I met in South Africa, who told me his father taught him the meanings of specific animal sounds, and particularly those of African birds. When this guide was trying to locate a leopard in the bush, for example, he looked to the flying direction and sounds of some of those birds. He told me the birds warned the other animals of a leopard's approach. He was the only guide, it was said, and who was always able to locate the elusive and solitary leopard.

The disastrous tsunami that devastated Southern Asia in the latter days of 2004, perhaps, could have been predicted by the region's animals, had people listened for them. As it turned out, very few animals were lost. They escaped before the tsunami hit, first sensing the initial earthquake under the Indian Ocean and immediately fleeing.

So, six rewrites on *After Marseilles*, and still counting. With a play it is never over until the play is published, and even then...

Since we now live in the computer age, I find it valuable to save the hard copies of all my drafts in addition to hard-drive and disc copies of several drafts. These recorded drafts represent the history of each play, as well as reminding us about the process of our rewriting. The professional writer knows that the first draft, after all, only represents the beginning.

Exercises

1 Take a current piece you are working on, after you have completed one draft and before you start the next draft. Make your own numbered list of what problems need to be dealt with in the next draft. Decide how you will accomplish the changes you

desire. Then methodically go through the script crossing off each change as you effect it.
2. Take a script or proposal you put away because it wasn't working. Make certain at least six months has elapsed since you put it down. Read it with fresh eyes. What could you do in a rewrite that might make it better, providing you still feel passionate about this project?
3. Take a dramatic project where you are indecisive about which character is the protagonist. Outline your project, first using Character A as the protagonist and then using Character B as the protagonist. The character with the strongest desire is more likely to go to the edge to get what he/she wants. Which character has the possibility of the more dramatic journey?

Assignment

Start attacking your rewrite list.
Deal with your first three rewrite notes.

Week 10
Adapting from fact, fiction, and further

The subjects of our screenplays, plays, and TV proposals often choose us. Something we have read or heard or seen or dreamt, or a place we've traveled to catches our imagination, doesn't let go, and we are off.

One of the things I've enjoyed about being a writer is the expansive and varied canvas for projects it's afforded in theater, film, and TV. In your career, the time will come when you are either commissioned or choose to adapt a novel, short story, or film for another genre. There will also be historical material that will attract you, or a book of non-fiction, or someone's life, or a real story that is brought to you or you read about and you believe will make a strong dramatic subject. The choice has to do with the medium you think best suits the telling of this story, helping it to shine.

The laws of public domain covering a current piece of work in the US are in effect for the entirety of the author's life plus seventy more years. Ideas or facts, however, are not covered under laws of copyright. No one can own a fact; but the particularized expression of that idea *is* covered and is inviolate. In that way, all authors own the exact placement of language in describing an idea.

In regards to the depiction of someone's life or a specific event, it is wise to get approval from the people involved or their agents, before you begin to write. Although anyone is entitled to write about any public person, according to Ralph Sevuch, current Associate Director for the Dramatists Guild of America, litigious claims often arise arguing everything from defamation of character to the omission of an important event or character in the person's life being represented. Because you are not a journalist, and are reconfiguring the real story in order to make your project worthy, you are always better off clearly owning the rights.

Adaptation from fact is the more popular form, as it allows for passions that originate with the author. There is a much larger opportunity for originality when adapting from fact, as challenging as adapting from fiction is. When adapting from fact, you do your research, do your interviews, and then it is up to you to formulate the story.

There is more room to maneuver in an original piece based on fact, whether it is founded on a particular incident or a period in history that serves as background for your project.

If you are adapting a short story or novel, do is the following:

- After reading the novel or short story, make a step-by-step outline of the plot.
- Next, list every character.
- Then, on a piece of graph paper, plot out the rising action of the short fiction or novel. What is the major dramatic incident? Is there one?
- Where will you choose to start? Is it a place already described in the novel or will you be constructing a new opening scene?
- Go through all forty questions to ask when writing a screenplay, play or when writing for TV (Chapter 5), determining which questions are answered in the piece of fiction as it is, and where the holes are.
- In rereading the book, what material will you choose to exclude? Why?

Now...

- Decide how you may choose to change the plot in order to increase the dramatic tension.
- Decide how many of the characters you plan to keep, keeping in mind practicalities. Who will you choose and why? Will you cut some characters? Which ones? Will you merge some of the characters? How?
- Construct a new plot outline, incorporating your choice of characters.
- Know approximately where you want to end the story, but wait until the actual writing, so your characters can lead you to the end.
- Understand that in some instances a piece of fiction may be adaptable while remaining generally faithful to the original text. If so, you are fortunate, but you do want to ask: why adapt this particular piece for stage if it has already been written for the printed page and even for film? What does a play, for example, do for a piece that few other mediums can accomplish, given the changing audience and performance every evening? I always think of screenplays as musical compositions, with each concert, conductor, location, and orchestra adding to the life of that piece.

Although it's more common to adapt a novel into film because of the availability of location and scope in a film, as well as the camera's ability to concentrate on the characters by the use of close-ups (thereby possibly utilizing the interior passages in a novel), there are several examples of successful adaptations of novel and short stories for stage. There are many more novels adapted into musicals for the stage, but here we are only discussing fiction into straight drama. Successful adaptations of fiction include Edward Albee's brilliant adaptation of Vladimir Nabokov's *Lolita*, Ruth and August Goetz's *The Heiress*, suggested by the Henry James novel *Washington Square*, and the recent fine adaptation by Peter Parnell of John Irving's novel *The Cider House Rules*. Perhaps one of the best examples of a classic novel adapted for the stage is John Steinbeck's *The Grapes of Wrath*.

The Grapes of Wrath, a Pulitzer Prize-winning novel, published in 1939, tells the story of a displaced farm family from Oklahoma who travel to California in search of a "promised land." They only want to work and live in dignity as a family, lead by Ma Joad. Their arduous journey to California, punctuated by death and desertion, is extended by travel between the migrant labor camps, while attempting to find meaningful and satisfying work. The family continues to suffer indignities, harassment, and outright persecution by corporate entities and local law enforcement, and they survive day to day, doing "what you have to do." Their spirit is sustained by an enduring belief in the connection between "common folk" for mutual support and benefit.

This basic story of a migrant farm family from the Dust Bowl in the midst of the Great Depression resonates through succeeding generations as a great American novel, and was a significant reason for Steinbeck receiving the Nobel Prize for Literature in 1962. The novel was made into a prize-winning film in 1940, scripted by Nunnally Johnson, directed by John Ford, and starring Henry Fonda as Tom Joad, the protagonist in the story. The theater director Frank Galati adapted the novel for stage and the Steppenwolf Theatre Company of Chicago first presented it in 1988. There were subsequent productions of the play at the La Jolla Playhouse in La Jolla, California and at the National Theatre in the UK, both occurring in 1989. In 1990, the play was produced on Broadway, directed by Frank Galati, and received a Tony Award as Best Play in that year.

The process of adapting a novel starts with an understanding of the multiple layers of the story and the character motivations. These inform the subsequent choices for dramatization of scenes to provide the spine of the dramatic piece and the emotional development of the characters. A first level in any drama is an individual character's interaction with other characters. In the introduction to the Penguin Books 1992 edition of *The Grapes of Wrath*, Robert DeMott quotes Louis Owens' explanation of biblical parallels in four of the five layers claimed by Steinbeck:

> On one level it is the story of a family's struggle for the survival in the Promised Land. On another level it is the story of a people's struggle, the migrant's. On a third level it is the story of a nation, America. On still another level, through... the allusions to Christ and those to the Israelites and Exodus, it becomes the story of mankind's quest for profound comprehension of his commitment to his fellow man and to the earth he inhabits.

This linear and profound novel presents a clear challenge to the adaptor, as the novel employs an unusual presentation of hard-hitting general information in chapters that alternate with longer chapters on the specific lives of the Joad family struggle. These general chapters act as a sort of Greek chorus to underline and expand the struggles and challenges of the migrant men and women. In fact, music has a prominent place in the novel for individuals and families, and the Saturday night dance at the Weedpatch Camp is the setting for a major confrontation. Frank Galati incorporates many of these general statements and emotions in song and music that separates, and provides transition to, the scenes involving the Joad family. Original music provided for the production included "The Dust Bowl Folk Song" and the "Car Salesmen Song." Music is also used to define and reinforce the action on the film—for example, the recurring musical theme that represents the engine of the Joad's dilapidated truck.

This illustrates the premise that a dramatic piece, no matter what script category, is more than just a sequence of speeches. The music, sound effects, setting, scenery, and costumes all contribute to the telling of the emotional story. The writer needs to consider all of these effects and identify, in the script, those elements necessary to propel the story and action. However, these effects should not overwhelm the characters, which must carry and deliver the emotional burden of the story. As Frank Galati points out in an author's note in the Dramatists Play Service edition of the script, the Steppenwolf ensemble once performed this play on a bare stage for an invited audience. He notes:

> The campfires of the migrants, the long trough of water (covered by a movable lid on the film apron) that served as both the Colorado River and the stream that flooded the box-car camp

and the sheets of rain that drenched the Joads near the end of the second act in Kevin Riddon's simple and elegant design for the production were present only in the imagination of the audience, and yet the grip of the story held tight.

The writer must hold tight to the emotion of the story, and for an adaptation of a novel, must learn as much as possible about the circumstances surrounding the novel, including the setting in time and place, the author's commentary, if any, and possible insights by reviewers. In the end, the writer must make choices in eliminating material and, possibly, entire scenes, or revising the sequence and actions of the novel. A novel often enjoys the luxury of length, description, repetition, and internal thoughts, and may introduce characters and events that enhance the story and provide supporting elaboration, but may not be essential to the emotional spine of the story. They may, in effect, be more decoration for the dramatic script than it needs.

Some examples from Galati's script illustrate this point. In the first chapter of the novel, Tom Joad hitches a ride with a truck driver on the way home from prison, where he has been released on parole from a seven-year sentence for killing a man. This introduces Tom and provides background for the times (the driver is violating company rules by picking up a rider). In the second chapter, Tom walks up the dusty dirt road towards home and finds Jim Casey, the preacher (now inactive, but still in demand), sitting under a tree. This introduces Casey, and he leaves with Tom for the old homestead. In the film version, the action starts with a bus stopping along a highway, and Tom alights and begins his walk up the dirt road. In the play, the action begins with Casey playing a little harmonica and then singing a church hymn. Tom enters the scene and the two begin the dialogue. Eliminating the scene with the truck driver does not diminish the initial thrust of the story, which is captured in the scene between Tom and Casey. The truck driver never appears again in the novel, but in the screenplay, for example, plays a major role in the story.

When Tom and Casey reach the severely damaged and abandoned homestead, Muley appears and adds to the development of the story, as well as illustrating the effect on an individual of being displaced from his livelihood. Muley will not leave his roots, even though he is hunted like the rabbits he hunts. In the novel, the three men skin, cook, and eat the rabbits Muley has bagged, although this activity is not included in the play. While it adds rich detail in the novel, it is not central to the action of the story, although Galati's script does include campfires as part of the fundamental elements of earth, fire, and water.

Similarly, there are other sections of the novel dropped from the play, including the sequence in which the Joads meet and join forces with the Wilsons along Route 66. This is a reinforcement of the theme and would only add length and characters to the piece.

A notable adjustment to the storyline occurs in the play script when Tom has apparently killed a man in response to Casey being beaten to death. In the novel, Tom's nose is broken in the fight and he must hide out near the boxcar camp while Ma sneaks him food until he heals and won't be easily recognized. Ruthie inadvertently tells of Tom's hiding and he must leave for good. In the play, Tom is similarly injured, but leaves immediately. The emotional separation of Tom and Ma Joad is just as moving and permits the action to proceed more directly. There are several scenes in the novel in which the Joads find some work picking peaches and cotton, but they are not dramatized in the play. Additionally, the young children are present in the play, but have very limited speaking roles; in the novel they speak often and illustrate the richness of the family's life together. In the adaptation from the novel to the script, adjustments to specific actions are often necessary to streamline the flow without losing the emotional thread. You should examine the texts of *The Grapes of Wrath* yourself, and determine if you agree with the choices and changes made, such that the play and screenplay maintain the novel's emotional backbone.

In beginning any adaptation from fiction, we are ultimately forced to select what and who will stay, who will be let go, and who will be added. The process is similar to the rewriting process in that you are concerned with insuring there is clarity, conflict, confrontation, resolution, tension, drama, and some ultimate change in your adaptation. You are looking at the way the author told the original story and deciding how *you* want to tell the story. Remember your adaptation is always "based on." You, the writer, either make a decision to be fairly faithful to the text or to re-imagine it. "Always try to see things in a new pattern," a former professor of mine at Brandeis, Jim Clay, would urge. As writers, we should always be trying to stretch. It's known as flexing your writing muscles.

For me, the process of adapting from fact is a more exciting prospect. Because we cannot always write solely out of our own bellies and hearts, there comes a time when we yearn for the framework and support of available facts. Sometimes, in doing the research, it is as if you are sifting through gold and fashioning from it a rich mosaic or linear story. It's as if you are a sculptor given the materials to which you must give the shape. In writing a dramatic piece that originates only out of your own imagination, no one supplies the material. In an adaptation, you mine the material.

QED is a play by American playwright Peter Parnell that chronicles part of a day in the life of Nobel Prize-winning physicist Richard Feynman. It presents scenes from a day in Feynman's life, less than two years before his death, interweaving many strands from Feynman's biography, from the Manhattan project to the Challenger inquiry to more personal topics such as the death of Feynman's wife, and his own fight with cancer. The play, which grew out of collaboration between Parnell, actor Alan Alda, and director Gordon Davidson, premiered in 2001. Parnell writes:

> With each draft we read, Alan got more and more depressed. He loved the character and what I was doing, but he knew we weren't getting to the heart of it. After about six drafts of the play and several years of working on the play, between TV series and other projects, I was about to give up when I finally thought "Why don't I just see what happens if I have Alan alone?"

The resulting one-man show was a combination of Feynman's words, his friend and editor Robert Layton's words, and the playwright's words, and its success has to do with Parnell's brave and right choice to incorporate a complex life into the one major character, and the choice to concentrate on the last part of his life as the center of the play. It is about selection, and as you can see, perseverance. The excitement is often in the process of figuring out how to tell the story.

In addition to biographical plays and screenplays, there are the strictly documentary ones, dealing with real people and the dramatization of their words. Recently, writers Jessica Blank and Erik Jensen pieced *The Exonerated* together from interviews. The play enjoyed a successful and astonishingly moving production at the 45 Bleecker Street Theatre in New York, under the auspices of The Culture Project. Their subject was men who had been on death row and were eventually exonerated.

In gathering the material for the project, the authors felt it was important to preserve the men's actual words as much as possible. They describe the process of gathering the interviews, court material, letters, poetry and other supporting documents, and then chipping away at the whole as sculptors, so the remaining play represented the question they were probing: what could have gone wrong in a court system that incarcerated men on death row who were not guilty?

114 *Adapting from fact, fiction, and further*

In adapting from fact, the dramatist's tasks are doubled. Not only do you have to select and condense the material you gather, as well as put it into a timeframe, but you have to attend to all the usual rules of any dramatic piece, including character, dialogue, conflict, confrontation, escalating plot, and an organic ending. In one form, writing a purely original drama, you are creating the pieces as you write. In adaptation, you first collect the pieces and then shape them into a script.

A few years ago, together with my husband Donald Wille, I wrote a spec screenplay based on the sinking in 1963 of the USS Thresher, a nuclear-powered navy submarine. My husband, a nuclear engineer, had worked with Admiral Rickover building the first naval submarine, and was at the commissioning of the Thresher. He knew the territory.

After a year of research, reading articles and books, and trying to piece together the mystery of why she sank, the US Naval Archives were opened and we were able to get the direct accounts and probable reasons for the failure. Armed with all these facts, we outlined a screenplay, with a backstory starting before the submarine took off on its final voyage, and set up some of the characters. We also decided to add a love interest. We didn't want a screenplay with all males. We established our characters and an outline, combining facts with imagination, including what we were beginning to think was the reason the Thresher sunk during sea trials. After an initial draft and four rewrites, we pitched the project to a well-known producer in Los Angeles. We chose him because he had been involved with film projects of moral inquiry.

The meeting was lively and he listened intently. When we finished presenting the project he finally spoke:

> I don't want to do a film where everybody dies at the end.

We didn't dare utter "But what about the Titanic?" because we didn't have Leonardo de Caprio signed on, and the producer had already risen from his chair.

Next, we brought the project to a New York producer who had done many dramas and documentary projects with HBO. He said he would be interested in the drama if it were written as a straight documentary. He didn't want to do a project that was part documentary and part fiction. Just the facts for him. I wish the end of this story was different, but, discouraged, we tucked the project in the bottom of a drawer where it still sits, sunk like the Thresher.

In the summer of 2015, a new musical, *Poster Boy*, based on the story of the young man who jumped off the George Washington Bridge in New York, was workshopped at Williamstown Theatre Festival. Its author was composer and lyricist Craig Carnelia. A former student, Joe Traze, wrote the book. It's based on the story of a young man who was harassed because of his sexual choice. His roommates spied on him, taking photos of his love affair with another young man, and posting them on the internet. This led to the young man's suicide. The authors had all the news stories and also secured interviews with some of the real people involved, including the young man's mother. They had the facts and imagined the rest.

Currently, I'm working on a screenplay about South Africa, based on my play *A Question of Country*. Part one takes place during the Apartheid period, from 1948 to 1986. Part two begins in 1986, continues through the election of Nelson Mandela as president (1994), and culminates with the hearings of the Truth and Reconciliation Commission (1998–2000).

The dramatic adaptation was generated by the story of a South African white woman and her struggles together with a group of Xhosa and Zulu women to form a grass-roots organization (Chapter 6).

The story, as told to me, presented a challenge, as it took place over 60 years, and involved hundreds of people and their stories; the material, however, was filled with drama and dealt with complex political issues.

How did the initial adaptation from a true story come together? First, arrangements were made for me to meet the real person the story was based on and get her approval to tell the story. She came to the US and gave her blessings, with one caveat. The story should not be solely about her, but about the women who worked with her in the grass-roots human-rights movement she started. I reassured her and the research began.

Within a few months I was off to Cape Town, where I stayed with the woman and her family, and was put into contact with dozens of people who had been active in organizing against apartheid. Since the founder was still working actively in post-apartheid South Africa, I was also able to follow her around every day and make trips to the outlying townships, as well as the many programs she had established. These included AIDS centers, programs for the elderly, pre-school programs, houses for orphans, programs for the blind, sports programs, and a small factory where a couple of dozen women, many disabled, sewed dolls and animals, which were sold worldwide to raise funds to help thousands still in need in the townships.

While in Cape Town, I recorded more than fifty interviews, including with people who had been actively involved in the apartheid regime, as well as with those who were part of the Truth and Reconciliation Commission

Armed with the interviews, I returned home, transcribed them, and then began the reading. As in the play about China, I gathered every book I could find on the history of South Africa, personal journals from the apartheid period, including Nelson Mandela's from Robben Island, books and documentaries about the Truth and Reconciliation Commission, including Alex Boraine's *A Country Unmasked*, and books about international truth commissions, including Patricia Hayner's *Unspeakable Truths*. In addition, there were materials at the Library of Congress, as well as documents filed with the South African Courts of Law. As I read, I summarized the major points from each document on large index cards.

The organization of the piece and actual writing happened a year later, at the Rockefeller Institute in Italy. Two boxes of notes and two cartons of books were mailed beforehand, ready for the work to begin.

As outlined in Chapter 6, at this point, some kind of structure started to take shape. As Lynn Ahrens, the lyricist for *Ragtime*, when interviewed for the *Dramatists Guild* quarterly, July/August 2015, said:

> With the novel of Ragtime, it's such a dense book: there are so many characters. Some are historical, some are fictional, and all their stories have equal weight. So we had to spend time with Terrence (the book writer, Terrence McNally) discussing which characters and stories to focus on.

For a long time I had heard the first line of the play in my head. It would be the woman whose life it was based on, and she would begin: "This story is not about me. Get that straight. Every woman was a Mama to Africa." With that I was off and wrote the first scene that was the actual genesis of the story, with the nurse and a township woman on the steps of Groote Schuur Hospital, holding a dead black baby, rolled up in a rug. From there the characters took over and began to write the scenes for me, sometimes following the outline, other times not. I knew what the last scene of Act 1 would be and knew what the very last scene in the play would be. Or I thought I did.

The process was like piecing together a giant jigsaw, with the joy of fitting all the parts into a coherent and moving story. It was thrilling. I could hardly breathe while writing it. The people and their stories were what this play was all about, and what any following adaptation for the film would encompass. All our struggles are heroic, and to be able to touch any one of them in your lifetime as a writer is a gift.

There is an additional kind of adaptation that I'll call "Postulation." The writer begins with a fact based on history, and then imagines either the backstory or the future. For example, in *King Charles III*, UK playwright Mike Bartlett imagines an unstable monarchy headed by Charles, immediately after the death of Elizabeth II, where Machiavellian maneuverings by both the royals and politicians force Charles to confront his own limitations. Written in iambic pentameter because the author believed that heightened form suited his subject matter, the play is Shakespearean in how it deals with ambition, power, and the conflicts occurring when you are thrust into a high position.

Lecture delivered to a graduate class in Adaptation at New York University's Tisch School of the Arts, Spring 2005, and at Beijing Film School, Fall 2014

Exercises

1 Choose a piece of fiction that has been adapted for both film and stage. Compare the original version with the two adaptations. Does one stand out as better than the others? Why?
2 Take one week's worth of daily newspapers and find a story in them you are interested in adapting. What kind of research would be required in order to adapt the story? Does the prospect excite you? Then you know you're onto something!
3 Choose an event, current or historical, that has always excited your curiosity. Remember most adaptations based on fact involve the writer in solving a mystery. You are often writing to find out why or how something happened. First isolate the questions you want to answer, and then go to those resources that may provide what you need. In this digital age, research is simplified… just Google and go.

Assignment

Continue your rewrite.

Week 11
Comedy

Humor is making fun of a character's dignity without letting him lose it.

Comedy essentially depicts our humanness, our vulnerability. We all try to do our best and often fail. Sometimes we do slip on the banana peel or walk into a door, devices often used in broad comedy.

Comedy is also about the unexpected. A naturally clumsy person walking into a door is not funny, but a pompous character bumping into an object is humorous. We also love seeing the person in a high position and with a sense of entitlement fall, because they are never expecting it. They assume they will win. The same goes for the bumbling villain, as played by Steve Buscemi in the film *Home Alone*, who is outwitted by an eight-year-old, as played by Macaulay Culkin. This comedic device is used, and often repeated in a single film. Even though we expect a certain behavior, once it is established, it becomes more laughable.

The repetition of anything that assaults a character's dignity depends on this repeat, because now the audience can see it coming. Our response is "Oh, oh, he's going to do it *again*," and we start to laugh before it even happens, enjoying our knowledge of what comes next. I call it the "just watch" syndrome. We congratulate ourselves on being on the inside track, recognizing "the expected."

Classical tragedy involved great heroes in a large fall from grace. Arthur Miller turned this theory on its head when he wrote *Death Of A Salesman*, about the common man suffering the precipitous fall. At the same time, Eugene O'Neill and later Joe Orton also left kings behind. In tragedy and tragi-comedy, the plot often involves an ordinary man/woman who rises in his station, only to bungle it in a large way, and then turn it right by the end, in an unexpected manner. This scenario is used in most romantic film comedies from *Bringing Up Baby* to *Four Weddings and a Funeral*, and the 2014 TV series *Vicious*.

Vicious is a BBC TV series about two aging gay men who have been living with each other fifty years, for better and worse. Created by playwright Mark Ravenhill and TV writer Gary Janneti, the predictability is part of the charm and comfort of the series. You know Freddie will say something to Stuart like "I see you're wearing an extra chin for the occasion," and Stuart will say something to Freddie, who wears a hearing aid, like "When the time comes, I'm going to so enjoy unplugging you." You know Ash will always stammer and blush and say something endearing, and that Violet will end up in full black leather, handcuffed to a bed in Argentina. And you may just laugh anyway.

No matter how outrageous, comedy should always begin in logic, be grounded in reality, and then make its own way to lunacy. Comedy comes out of our ability to laugh at our foibles. It is a way of bringing up an important issue by coming up and over, rather than frontally, or in a straightforward manner.

Some of us who write comedy undervalue it in the mistaken belief it isn't serious writing. But comedy is the hardest thing to teach. To successfully write comedy, you either have a sense of humor or not. It is a way of looking at the world. I have never been able to teach someone to be funny. The exception is the TV sitcom where the comedy sometimes comes out of set-up jokes, and this *can* be learned.

Humor can often be the most effective vehicle for a serious subject. Why? Because it's in opposition to the geometric theorem that a straight line is the shortest distance between two points.

A straight line is the last thing comedy demands. It wants to be slightly off the norm, and when exaggerated, way off the rule. What follows is an example.

The idea was to write a play about divorce, based on personal experiences. In reality, the legal process had been "nuts," and once the machinery was going, even if you had changed your mind, there was no stopping. It was as if you were on a fast-moving assembly line. It made me think of Lucy and Ethel trying to keep up with the conveyer belt at the candy factory.

Divorce is a serious subject, and I started out, tackling it as any writer would a tragedy; however, no matter what way I tried to tell the story, it bored me. Then I thought of the film *Divorce Italian Style* and it started to become clear. Some of the absurdity of the process was more suited to farce and made its point better without melodrama or didacticism.

This is from a scene towards the end of *The Agreement* (published by Broadway Play Publishing, March 2000), when the settlement is whizzing by.

CHARACTERS

Sybil Matchett

Sigmund Matchett

Alice Bailey—Sybil's lawyer

Lester Ostermeyer—Sigmund's lawyer

LESTER

To him, all statuary.

ALICE

To her, all paintings.

LESTER

To him, all loose lamps.

ALICE

To her all fixed lighting.

LESTER

To each, all gifts from the other's family.

ALICE

He gets to keep the French oriental.

SYBIL

Sigmund doesn't even *like* the French Oriental

SIGMUND

I didn't even know we *had* a French Oriental

SIGMUND

Why don't you ask her about the time she and her friends from WAM put a live rabbit in the bed.

SYBIL

Simply to remind you of *your* responsibility in the birth control process.

ALICE

And on the insurance, he had the dismemberment amendment, God forbid.

LESTER

God forbid.

SIGMUND

God forbid!

ALICE

So on this twenty-fifth day of August, the part of the first part agrees with the party of the second part...

LESTER

You're really getting a fine agreement, Dr Matchett. Everything spelled out.

ALICE

Everyone goes away happy. (Handing them some papers) Now if you'll both sign this paper, you could be divorced this afternoon. This agreement will not be considered final, of course, for six months; so both of you would have to wait that period to remarry.

LESTER

People are waiting to lock up.

ALICE

Your signatures please.

(They both sign)

ALICE

AND IT'S OVER!

LESTER

It's over Dr Matchett!

SYBIL

Wait a minute! You forgot the children!

LESTER

The children.

ALICE

The children.

SIGMUND

How could you forget the children?

ALICE

Well they're *your* children.

LESTER

You could have reminded us. So he gets the children, no strings attached.

SYBIL

Wait a minute I'm not giving up any children.

LESTER

We all have to make do with partial rewards.

ALICE

I move we put the children on a Rider.

LESTER

Ride the children.

In the 1980s, the Manhattan Punchline Theater (MPT), run on a shoestring and a dime by Steve Kaplan, produced some of the best comedy in the country. Steve gave many of us our start, giving *The Agreement* a hilarious production. Oliver Platt goes on to say in a *New York Magazine* interview about MPT:

> In 1986, I was a member of the comedy core of the Manhattan Punchline Theater, an off-off-Broadway theater on Theater Row. If you answered the phones and swept the floor you could audition for their plays. (When you're a new actor, the big catch-22 is that you can't get a job without an agent and you can't get an agent without a job, and so the right to audition for something when you've just gotten here is a treasured commodity.)

Steve had a keen eye for talent, and in 1987 produced *All in the Timing* by a young David Ives, master of the short form, who went on to write many full lengths, including *Venus in Fur*, and who was nominated for a Tony for a translation of Georges Feydeau's *A Flea in Her Ear*. My favorite Ives's piece has remained *Words, Words, Words*, about three chimpanzees, Swift, Kafka, and Milton, trying to write an original piece. At the end, Kafka comes up with the opening of *Hamlet*, typing, *Act one, scene one. Elsinore Castle, Denmark...*

There are different categories in comedy. Let's begin with:

FARCE, i.e. exaggeration, absurdity, ridiculous situations where chaos reigns and escalates, as in Michael Frayn's *Noises Off*, the operettas of Gilbert and Sullivan, Feydeau's *A Flea In her Ear*, and in Stanley Kubrick's film *Dr Strangelove*. The opening of Ionesco's *The Bald Soprano* establishes the farcical tone clearly:

MRS SMITH

There, it's nine o'clock. We've drunk the soup, and eaten the fish and chips, and the English salad. The children have drunk English water. We've eaten well this evening. That's because we live in the suburbs of London and because our name is Smith.

Taylor Mac's recent play *Hir* deconstructs the family drama better than anything since Thornton Wilder's *The Skin of Our Teeth*. Can you categorize it as farce? Yes, in the best sense of the drama of absurdity. You are laughing at first, then stung in the heart by knives and arrows.

SATIRE: societal or political scorn that ridicules or mimics. Its purpose is having the audience grasp just how low a segment of society crawls. Satire has the capability of being the harshest of all the comedy forms. It's fueled by anger. If I wanted to bring someone down, that's what I would use. Brecht's *Mother Courage* opens in 1624, when a sergeant and a recruiting officer draft soldiers for a war in Poland. When the officer complains how difficult it is to recruit from the lazy townspeople, the recruiting officer says the town could use a good war. He claims it will organize the people into action. Mother Courage has been profiting by war all along, following the armies of the Thirty Years' War, supporting herself and her children with her canteen wagon. Ironically, she sees her children's deaths from the beginning, foretelling their fates in Scene 1. Each will die because of the war Courage profits from.

PARODY: mirroring another writer's style for the sake of ridicule. One of the best is Mel Brooks' parody of the Wild West, *Blazing Saddles*. From the film:

HEDLEY LAMARR

I want you to round up every vicious criminal and gunslinger in the west. Take this down. I want rustlers, cut throats, murderers, bounty hunters, desperados, mugs, pugs, thugs, nitwits, halfwits, dimwits, vipers, snipers, con men, Indian agents, Mexican bandits, muggers, buggerers, bushwhackers, hornswogglers, horse thieves, bull dykes, train robbers, bank robbers, ass-kickers, shit-kickers and Methodists.

TAGGART

(Finding pen and paper)

Could you repeat that, sir?

PHYSICAL COMEDY: the most common manifestation of physical comedy is slapstick. It involves bodily and visual gags like wacky chases, pie throwing, and falls. The term "slapstick" comes from the name of the prop that performers would use to hit each other for comic effect. Charlie Chaplin is one of the most renowned slapstick comedians of the twentieth century, along with The Three Stooges and the Marx Brothers. The origins of slapstick can be traced back to the Italian Renaissance, with the emergence of *commedia del' arte*. It was grounded in athleticism and used archetypal clown characters. The screwball comedies that arose in 1930s combine the emphasis on physicality and sight gags of slapstick with social satire. The plots of these comedies often revolve around misunderstandings and focus on romantic relationships.

George Meredith, a major Victorian novelist and poet, wrote a definitive essay on comedy in 1877. Meredith said the comic poet is in the "enclosed square of the society he depicts" and that the "comic idea enclosed in a comedy makes it more generally perceptible and portable, and that is an advantage." He also wrote "The satirist is a moral agent, often a social scavenger, working on a storage of bile." He went on to say:

> You may estimate your capacity for comic perception by being able to detect the ridicule of those you love without loving them less; and more by being able to see yourself somewhat ridiculous in dear eyes, and accepting the correction their image of you proposes.

In his "Essay on Comedy," Wylie Sypher, a former professor and English department chair at Simmons College, Boston, writes that man's calamities seem to prove that human life at its depth is inherently absurd. He goes on to say, "We laugh in self-defense, and to ease our aching sense of inferiority." He cites Schopenhauer, who claimed laughter represents the "sudden perception of incongruity between our ideals and the actualities," and Byron's line "I laugh at any mortal thing/ Tis that I may not weep."

Authors examine the use of comedy in dramatic writing

Mark Ravenhill

Playwright: *Shopping and Fucking, Some Explicit Polaroids, Mother Molly's Clap House*

British and American comedy writing has often flourished when fresh waves of immigration open up the language for new forms of comic invention. Comedy in English is frequently expressed in language, from the puns and wordplays of Shakespeare's comedies to the wisecracks and cross-talk of contemporary sitcoms. We expect our comic characters to say funny things, be it Rosalind in *As You Like It* or Rachel in *Friends*.

But Molière's comedy is rarely expressed through the clever language his characters use. Molière was writing at a time when the French language was becoming centralized, codified. A simple but elegant use of the language was valued above extended vocabulary and the slipperiness of wordplay. It is this simplicity that has made Molière difficult to translate: sentences which have an ease and elegance in French can seem just too simple, almost "naked" in English.

Today, teams of writers work away to "punch up" our television and film comedies so that every line is a zinger and characters compete to wisecrack their way out of every situation. But today's comedy writers could learn from the simplicity of Molière's language and comic plotting, which allows for the humanity of his characters to breathe. And for the audience, through laughter, to share that humanity.

Molière's comedies don't make use of subplots and crazy plot twists. They follow just one clear plot in which eight characters or so (often members of a bourgeois family) each has a stake. The plot moves along with a lightness and a certain speed, without ever accelerating to the manic tempo of high farce or screwball comedy.

And in all of Molière's comedy is a sense of an underlying order. Human beings distort their actions by becoming obsessive—greedy for money or taken in by religious fervor—and this pulls them, and those around them, into irrational situations at which an audience laugh. But there is a balanced, human course of action open to them if they can only be cured of their obsessions. Molière laughs at the follies of human beings rather than criticizing his society. But his 'underlying order' is inclusive. It is not the order of the patriarchal male but one that all people have in common. Molière is a humanist.

Jenny Lumet

Screenwriter: *Rachel Getting Married*

The most important element in comedy is absolute fearlessness. If you show an iota of fear, apology or permission seeking, you're done. Also, as a personal preference, it's more about a totally original perspective than any tearing down. Or if you're going to tear something down, build something better in its place. That's all I know. (Kreplach are funny! Kale is not! Go figure.)

Tina Howe

Playwright: *Birth and Afterbirth, Painting Churches, Coastal Disturbances, Pride's Crossing*

If you grow up in a house filled with language—your father writing and broadcasting the evening news on CBS radio and your mother enthusing over how scintillating the conversation was at the Gunther's dinner party the night before—nothing is funnier than when the words stop and physical comedy erupts. People going berserk and falling down.

So our Saturday afternoon pilgrimages to see Marx Brothers movies at the Trans Lux were both a guilty pleasure and incredible relief. We knew every reel by heart and would laugh ourselves liquid at their pratfalls. The true vaudevillians like Charlie Chaplin, Buster Keaton, and the Marx Brothers are anarchists. They shatter our sense of reality and nothing, but nothing is funnier than watching the height of lunacy they reach as they struggle to put it back together again.

More than once our high-minded family was ejected from the theater for making such a disturbance.

David Ives

Playwright: *All in the Timing, Venus in Fur*

Comedy? It's a mystery. Just like tragedy.

Phyllis Nagy

Playwright, screenwriter: (plays) *Rising, Butterfly Kiss, The Strip, Disappeared*; (screenplays) *The Talented Mr Ripley, Mrs Harris, Carol*

As an undergrad, I was too timid to publicly disagree with the prevailing opinions on funny plays and screenplays that were being shown to me as masterpieces of comic script writing. While others laughed at what I felt were obvious jokes (and could write their own, while I stumbled over them)—or broad humor, something with which I've never gotten on—I'd cower in corners wondering if the joke would perpetually be on me. And then I took a workshop with Len Jenkin. At the time, Len was working on an immensely funny adaptation of Franz Kafka's magnificent short story, "A Country Doctor." He shared his process with us, invited us to look beyond the bare bones of plot and find the keys to comedy: character, character, character—plus a bit of circumstance and a great deal of tone. On its surface, "A Country Doctor" is not a barrel of laughs. But Len truly opened my eyes to the fact that this is the entire point of comedy that matters—the funniest characters do not know they are funny, nor do they necessarily recognize the enormity of the rocks they push up hills. The best comedy tears you apart and fills you with a thrilling fear of recognition—while making you laugh at yourself as well as the circumstances of the characters whose lives are being dissected.

Polly Stenham

Playwright: *That Face, Tusk Tusk*

[She cited the band Radiohead, fronted by Thom Yorke, as an inspiration during the writing of her play *Tusk Tusk*.] Comedy plays almost a musical element. It can control the rhythms and pacing of an audience's emotional response by how you entwine comedy and tragedy. If you have a funny moment, you can often push a dark moment much further afterwards because comedy relaxes an audience. Cavemen and women used the sound of laughter to indicate it was safe to go to a certain area. A writer can use laughter to create a sense of safety then subvert it, which renders the subversion much more powerful then if it came from a more ordinary point in the scene.

Ryan Craig

Playwright: *The Happy Savages, The Holy Rosenbergs, Small Town Saturday Night*

Sometimes with me, almost every time, the comedy happens by accident. It happens when I'm trying to write something true. The humour's a bi-product of that truth, because it's an essential component part of our psychological make-up. It's where we go in our darkest hour, when we're broken; a signifier of our humanity. Sometimes you can be on the razor's edge with it. I encountered quite a bit of resistance when I wrote *The Holy Rosenbergs* for the National Theatre because of this. The play's set entirely on the evening of the funeral of the family's eldest son; an evening where the family's tearing itself apart politically as well as emotionally. I wrote the play very quickly, so what came out was quite raw, quite unconscious, and there was a lot of humor. Not because I was trying to write a comedy, but because I was trying to write the situation as honestly as I could; trying to explore how human beings behave when they're vulnerable, when they're in extremis, when they're hurting, when there's little hope, when the world is dark and cruel and violent and hostile and conspiring against you. If you're writing truthfully about those things, you're writing comedy.

Judith Johnson

Playwright: *Uganda, Goodbye Barcelona, Every Breath, Working Away*

Setting out to "write comedy" is something I've never done. I hardly dare acknowledge that I am actually trying to do it at all. It's like kissing someone when you don't really want to, you have to close your eyes and pretend it's something else. Sometimes, by chance, the kiss will actually hit home, it will be a pleasant surprise, and you may even enjoy it. Just like sometimes, when you're not expecting it, and quite against the odds, you actually come out with something funny.

Steve Kaplan

Director, producer, writer: (book) *The Hidden Tools of Comedy*

When comedy works

First off, let's differentiate between funny and comic.

Funny is whatever makes you laugh. Period. End of story. When my niece was five, I could shake a set of keys in her face, and dissolve her into hysterics. To her, that was funny. But is it comedy? Would you submit a set of keys to Sundance, or shake them in a comedy club, or show a picture of them in a book?

Funny is subjective. Different things make different people laugh at different times. To try to guess what other people find funny is a mugs game.

So if funny is subjective, what's comedy?

Freud thought is was man laughing at other's misfortunes. Bergson thought is was the "mechanical encrusted on the living." E.B. White said, "Analyzing humor is like dissecting a frog. Few people are interested and the frog dies of it." They all may be right, but I think that comedy is the art of telling the truth about what its like to be human. Drama might help us dream about what we could be, but comedy helps us live with who we are. And who are we?

We're a motley crew, hurtling through the void, in a cold, uncaring universe, not knowing where we came from, not knowing where we're going, trying out best in our fumbling, bumbling human way, to make each and every moment in that universe as good as we possibly can, or just a little bit better than the moment before. We're a species who continue to get up after being knocked down, either because we're too stupid or stubborn or hopeful to continue to stay down where it's safe, and where we'll all end up anyway.

It's stupid, futile, and hopeless. But no matter how hopeless we are, how pitiful, how pathetic, how wrong headed, how selfish, how petty our solutions, it's also wonderfully, gloriously human. And the comedian is simply the courageous man who gets up in front of a large group of strangers and admits to being human—telling the truth about himself, and others. People may be sitting the dark, thinking, "I'm a failure, I'm defeated, I'm all alone." The comic artist goes out there and says, "Me too." The essential gesture of the comedian is the shrug. "Hey, you'll live. I've been there, that's life, You'll live!"

The art of comedy is the art of hope. This is the truth, the comic metaphor for our lives.

So how does it work? Comedy tells a story about an ordinary guy or gal, struggling against insurmountable odds, without many of the required tools with which to win, yet never giving up hope!

Tell a story like that, and even though some people may not laugh, that's comedy.

Rajiv Joseph

Playwright, TV writer: (plays) *Animals out of Paper, Bengal Tiger at the Baghdad Zoo, The Guards at the Taj*; (TV) *Nurse Jackie*

The funniest thing I ever wrote on *Nurse Jackie* wasn't a line of dialogue and it wasn't even funny. It was a stage direction, and it was pretty simple: "Zoey begins to dance." But I knew it would be funny because the brilliant actress who played Zoey, Merritt Wever, is brilliantly funny. And I knew that when she began to dance, she would make comedic gold out of it. So this is my advice for writing comedy: write it for really funny people. And find those moments when they would do something totally unexpected and whimsical. Make them do it. Write those stage directions, and watch them do something hilarious. And then take credit for it.

Zack Udko

Playwright: *Scary Nation, Claw of the Schwa, Stranger in the Night*

   Comedy is a celebration of our collective anguish, anxiety, and inability to communicate with one another. Most comedies culminate in a comforting resolution, reminding us our flaws are not unique and that we are not alone. While tragedy encourages us to accept our inadequacies and failures, comedy solves problems and offers us opportunity to grow and move beyond obstacles.

Julia Brownell

Playwright, TV writer: (plays) *Cookie, All-American*; (TV) *Hung, Parenthood, About a Boy*

   When I was in college and doing improv I read the book *Truth in Comedy*, by Charna Halpern, Del Close, and Kim Howard Johnson, and it's something I still remind myself all the time. A well-defined character (specificity is key! specifics are funny!) just being him or herself is much funnier than a joke. I never set out to write funny; I set out to write characters that want things and get in the way of other characters that want things. This is dramatic conflict, but it's also often comedic.

Exercises

1 Identify three comedies—one each for theater, film, and TV. How would you categorize each one according to genre?
2 What is the best comic scene in each and why?

Assignment

Where can you utilize comedy in your script? Choose one scene. Rewrite it.

   Continue rewriting, referring to Chapter 9. A reminder: your completed script is due for Class 14—the last class.

Week 12
The habits of successful dramatic writers

To create means to fill a space that formerly went unused in the universe. For the writer, the world of ideas corresponds to the heavens. We sleep under the light of stars, the light of stars that have long since ceased to exist, and we pattern the actions of our characters on a reality which we create and ceases to exist outside the text and its performance. Our work lives on the stage, screen, and on the page. Early on, as writers, we learn the law of certainty is not certain at all. Yes, if we toss a coin in the air, 50 percent of the time it will fall on heads and 50 percent of the time on tails, but only if we toss the coin into infinity. In our lifetime we will not see this law of averages play itself out.

Success is not promised for any writer. The best we can do is practice habits that don't guarantee success but at least augur well for it. We do the best we can in an uncertain world. We run down the center of the road well armed, clear that the slings and arrows of both good and bad fortune will hit us; what we don't do is hide in the bushes where nothing has the chance of hitting us. The writer is out on the road observing, and endures by being a warrior and sustaining a financial reality. The days of the starving artist in the garret in the attic are over.

As an educator of thousands of dramatic writers, as well as witnessing my colleagues on the Dramatists Guild Council, I have witnessed those habits that appear to be common to successful writers for theater, film, and TV.

If Freud was correct that our satisfaction comes from a combination of triumph in love and work, and if Norman O. Brown is accurate in identifying the ultimate success as work that becomes a joy, then success is becoming the best of who we are and locating and embracing our uniqueness.

In all the years of teaching I have never encountered the same voice twice—dozens of love stories, countless efforts of characters to escape their beginnings, hundreds of wrong steps which lead to an excess of misfortune, numerous Oedipus-like stories where we watch the hero ride the waves naïvely to his or her own destruction. No one voice is like another. We are, as J. Brownowski points out in *The Identity of Man*, "machines at birth but individuals through experience."

Writing for an audience is a moral as well as an intellectual challenge. How we act, not what we say, shapes our identity as serious writers. The writer is simply one who piles up the pages. That is the true fabric of our being. Someone can say all they want "I am a writer," but character is action, and we, as the creators, know the truth of our dailiness. Our success lies in the deep habits of that dailiness—the truth when we get into bed with ourselves in the deep of the night, and who we truly are, how we really live our lives, not how we say we do.

Some of the habits of highly successful dramatic writers are as follows.

Focus

Focus infers a clear vision of the project you are writing, a centering and entering process—going for the very heart of the question you are asking. We write, as Joan Didion states, to discover what it is we are writing about. If it's an original piece or an adaptation, it's helpful to understand the generating moment for the idea, because we want to keep coming back to it, like a homing pigeon. It delivers the roots of the work and so clues us to the focus, reminding us of it.

If you are part of a writing team for a TV series, episodes either stand alone, such as *Law and Order SVU*, or are part of an ongoing season, where you are tracing the characters and story arcs, such as *House Of Cards*. Robert Cohen, a former student and now a writer on staff for *Law and Order SVU*, notes that the three to five writers in his group usually establish the focus of each episode, and from that, make a detailed outline, followed by index cards describing each scene, in order. Finally, before the writing begins, they do a "beat sheet." This sequences the story, using bullets, and is simply a condensed and focused way of looking at the story line. Television writing follows a pattern more than any other kind of dramatic writing. The focus is fully known at the start.

In other dramatic forms, one begins writing with an amorphous oozing ball in your hands. You then take a bat to it and hit it again and again until it becomes harder and smaller and you can hold the essence of your project in one hand. Call it theme, call it spine, but focus your attention on it. I often write the focus of my piece, once I get it, on a card and hang it above my computer.

Also, above my computer is a permanent index card reading "No one asked you to be a writer." This keeps me honest and in line. It also decreases the tendency to complain.

The index card for the focus of a recent project reads "The Necessity of Forgiveness." The previous project was "a gift is only a gift if someone can afford to accept it."

By keeping the center of the dramatic script clearly in sight, the writer is trying to hold to the backbone of the piece, and not take side trips into the lush countryside. No script can be about the entire world. I call it the "Stuffing one hundred pounds into a five-pound bag syndrome" when a writer does that.

So, find the center and stay there. Find the question you are positing with each dramatic piece. This works the same when you are developing a pilot for TV. Some of the questions I have asked in projects are as follows:

- Should we forgive violent actions?
- Should the victim forgive the perpetrator?
- What is the nature of evil?
- Can you impose love?
- How far will we go in the name of friendship when our private desires are called into play?
- Where is the separation between parent and child?
- How can you know a country simply by studying its history?
- Is giving always an act of kindness? What if the receiver cannot afford to accept something because the personal price is too high?
- How do we recognize love?

Focus also means keeping to a writing schedule. Mark it out in your calendar. It doesn't matter what time of day, or how long, or where. I know one writer who writes one page a day. That's his rule. If he exceeds his expectations, that's a spectacular day. This writer completes at least 365 pages a year. In a good year he writes two projects or one with six rewrites. But he is regular and keeps to his schedule.

Passion

Passion is what sustains perseverance. You must believe that what you are writing must be written. The same as you have to know what your characters will fight for and how far they will go, you have to believe you would go to the mat for this script, like a parent for a child. You have to believe that you are the only one in the world who could tell the story. An old friend, writer Eve Merriam, passed on this piece of wisdom to me and I never forgot it. Write from your greatest strength and fervor.

One time I began a play at the suggestion of an artistic director of a regional theater. The subject—the life and loves of an eminent American playwright—was fascinating, with opportunities for research into the personal life of this writer through her letters and interviews. The subject had never been done, and was eminently commercial. It would be hard to believe this project would not excite any living playwright. It was about Lillian Hellman and Dashiel Hammett.

Once the rights to the material were received, it was time to begin. But the more research I did through the archives at UT Austin, and the more I learned, the less I was in love with the subject. It remained a great idea, but not for me. The director who had suggested the subject called to ask, "Do you hear the play singing yet?" "No," I replied, "but that will come." Well, it never did sing. So, after six months of work, many scenes outlined and written, but no fire from inside, I abandoned the project and never looked back.

Someone else eventually wrote the project as a TV biopic, starring Sam Shepard and Jessica Lange, but I was grateful it wasn't me. Write from the heart. Believe in the fire. It's what delivers the work. It keeps you honest. Passion comes from our strongest beliefs and questions, those things in our society which anger us, those patterns of human behavior that betray the soul out of greed, jealousy, sheer opportunism, and ambition. Passion requires conviction and conviction demands a moral stance. Know what you stand for and have your characters do battle in its name.

A room of your own

To be a writer means you have a space you keep sacred for your work. A room of your own is a place where you write that makes you feel safe and the most productive. Is it in one location? Or are you a fan of Starbucks or Stumptown? Or do you prefer the lobby of a hotel? Do you need music, the noise of the city, or just birds and you? Do libraries work? Large reading rooms like the Copley Square Library in Boston or the one in the British Museum?

Virginia Woolf in *A Room of One's Own* is speaking in response to centuries of women who were "locked out" of "writing rooms" because of sociological and economic pressures. But women are not alone in being "locked out" in the twenty-first century. There are those denied entry to certain rooms either because of ethnicity, economics, social status, or gender. Then there are those of us who deny ourselves the benefit of a place, and usually, because of questions of entitlement—we don't think we deserve a room of our own. Take note of the Writer's Army, initiated by playwrights Anne Washburne and Madeleine George and based on a model by writer Eric Ehn, who has led several silent writer retreats. The Writer's Army creates one week (9am–1pm, 2pm–5pm daily) of a low-cost (usually US$50), silent, distraction-free writing space (they vary from session to session), coffee included (bring your own snacks). No cell phones allowed. Cheers to Anne and Madeleine.

Whether in a public space or a corner of a table in your apartment, claim it, fill it with your amulets and the necessary writing materials (no cheap pens that may leak, please), then set your sacred schedule and keep to it.

A clear understanding of the process

Writers who are successful understand our careers have topography. Only when we have come to the end of our days can we see the shape of a whole career, how it adds up. And this is the thing—it all counts, but the shape of each of our paths differs as much as the shape of our bodies.

Recently, I had occasion to name three alumnae awards at New York University. When I identified one playwright for the award she was shocked. "You don't want me," she said. "I'm not famous like the others who are getting the awards. I just have this tiny stuff done in teensy theaters no one ever heard of." But she was wrong. She had maintained a constant presence in the theater at small experimental theaters across the country. She was working in the theater and ten readings finally did lead to a production in New York and TV work. Trust the process of your own path and don't look to anyone else's pattern.

Having a clear understanding of the process also means the craft. We are always lost. As writers our job is to be lost. We start out knowing nothing but the glimmer of an idea. The world of one piece cannot prepare us for the world of the next. We are always explorers, breaking fresh ground and there are no certain answers.

Expect to be lost until you find your way and then lose it again. At the same time, do not mythologize craft. There are governing rules that are common to all good drama: a character has to be in a different place at the end of the story than at the beginning, obstacles have to escalate, one scene must push the next scene forward, and, if it's non-linear, the audience or reader has to be able to connect the scattered dots.

Perseverance

The race belongs not always to the swiftest or the most talented. Nothing is as heartbreaking as to watch a writer of medium talent persevere, believe in himself above everything, and subsequently outrun the more talented writer who does not have the stamina to stay in the race. This is not a battle to win, but one to remain true to yourself and your vision. If you decide writing is not for you, then stop and become what you really want. If you want to be a writer, there will be no cheerleaders at your back. Be determined to write the best you can, and about something that catches your passion, and then do battle.

Living as a warrior

As a writer you are going into combat every day. That's why you have to live as though you are in training. Get enough sleep. Exercise. Eat healthy. Don't lead a social life that is killing you; and as one warrior writer friend wisely stated, "don't piss it away on meeting someone for lunch." If you believe in the connectedness of mind and body, this is a purely intellectual profession that requires physical stamina and clarity. Save the best of yourself for your work. The legend of the dissipated writer is much overrated. Be firm and put your writing unquestionably first, or you will surely find it is the very last thing you get to.

Set deadlines

Writing a play, screenplay, or a spec TV pilot, including your rewrites, is a long process. Most plays and screenplays take three to five years. My own experience with spec pilots is anywhere from one month to one year. There *is* the author who miraculously writes an entire script in a month. Is it a polished version? It's unlikely. I have found it best *not* to write a first draft in the morning and then polish it in the afternoon. You need a breathing period, short or long. It often works if you wait just one day.

Self-motivation is crucial, set deadlines and meet them. I do not totally encourage this idea, but many a time I scheduled a reading of a first draft way before the script was completed. This absolutely gave me a deadline.

Rewriting as opportunity

The most experienced writers see rewriting as a chance to make the script better, to edit, to make it lean and mean, to pin emotional moments down to paper like a butterfly, and to make every line integral to the character or the plot.

We have to learn to listen, hear the fat and excise it, as well as to hear the missing beat and write it in. We must, as one critic told me at the beginning of my career, "want to hold on to your script as a mother would a child. Oh let me have it just for a while longer and I will make it better." Remember, you are batting around that oozing ball until it is hard as truth.

Take on large themes and paint a complex canvas

If we want to raise the stature of the arts, we have to tackle difficult questions. It requires us as writers making a clear work of art about complex subjects. We live in a universe that often eludes meaning and it is the writers who have to question it. If not the artist, then whom?

Emotional verity

A graduate student recently presented this problem: he knew how to construct plot and how to write dialogue, but how do you write emotions so they are believable?

The answer is simply that the writer is a schizophrenic. You must become each character emotionally as they speak. You must change your persona with every speech. That's a lot of twisting and turning, but verity depends on this individuation and also the taking on by the author of the emotional substructure of the scene.

If it is a scene about humiliation, we have to go back to those moments when we were actually humiliated. And if the scene is about falling in love, then it requires going back to that moment of rapture, or the moment, if called for, of rage or betrayal or utter disappointment or rejection, by pinning the feeling to a piece of our own emotional past. This explains why we feel so drained at the conclusion of writing certain scenes. Love is easy, losing is not.

Be professional

Rejection is not personal. I know it feels that way, but it is a matter of someone wanting what you have to sell. It takes only one producer to like your work and many to turn you down. You don't work with a director or a designer because they are your friends. It has to be a matter of who is best for your work. For the serious writer, it is always a case of the work. Concentrate on giving your work the best life—the life it deserves.

Imposing the plot

Plot is not a matter of artistic inspiration. Don't depend on the muses for your plot. Plot is simply mechanical. It is a means of testing the characters, causing them to change, heightening the drama, and keeping things moving. Plot is a moving story. It has nothing to do with art and everything to do with escalating obstacles—first this happened, which leads to this happening, which leads to the next happening, followed by the moment of highest action, after which everything is changed and there is no going back.

If you don't want to deal with plot, write poetry and talk about the moonlight coming through the trees. And if you want to take your time with the action and stop along the way to watch the sunset spreading over the hills, write a novel. In a dramatic piece there is no time to stop. Keep on pushing. You are on the road.

Aggressive marketing

Be aggressive with marketing your work, agent or not. No one will take care of your work as much or as well as you will. Yes, an agent will do it, but you are not their only client. Your agent may be enthusiastic, your friends may be supportive or not, and your mother may pledge her undying belief in you, but the thing that matters in the dark of the night is you and your own belief that someone out there will want your work.

As it turns out, the life of a dramatic script is very long and it may flow and ebb. The project may appear in California, be quiet for a while like a hibernating bear, then wake up in London, then go to sleep again and turn up in Seattle. Everyone says after those Seattle reviews, it is going straight to Broadway. But it goes instead to Cincinnati, and then shows up in Singapore, only to come back to New York via Munich, and after that, who knows? The life of the script is forever and no one can predict its full path. Not even Sophocles could.

Also, never apologize for calling or writing a theater or film company or producer to inquire about your script. They are in the business of producing writers' work, so you are whom they need. You are their best clients. Gear yourself up and make the call: "Hello, this is Orson Welles, and my friend Herman Mankiewicz and I were just inquiring as to the whereabouts of the script for *Citizen Kane* we sent you." Go forth and conquer.

And finally

1 Get up.
2 Make a pot of coffee.
3 Feed your animal. If you don't have one, buy one. And if you write in the morning don't get dressed until your writing period is through. In other words, live a totally evolved existence... read, have friends, go out for dinner, go to the gym, go on a trip, drive to the store, meditate, levitate, celebrate. Be totally engaged in life, which is our material, our landscape, our feeding ground, our nourishment, and our teacher.

In conclusion

Focus, passion, living as a warrior, a room of your own, a clear understanding of process, tackling complex themes and growing in your reach, imposing the plot, emotional verity, setting deadlines, rewriting as opportunity, professionalism, aggressive marketing, and a total engagement in life.

Nothing is guaranteed—not health nor wealth, not beauty nor power, not the Pulitzer Prize nor a British Academy Film Award, nor an Emmy, nor an Academy Award, but honor and grace is a choice in each of our lives. Being who we say we are gives us the best opportunity to be a success, and become what we want to be, embracing what we accomplish in our lifetime.

Lecture delivered to members of the Dramatist's Guild of America, Los Angeles, California, February 2001

Exercises

1 Post an index card in your workspace stating the focus of the piece you are currently working on. State it in one or two sentences.
2 In a notebook list two possible future projects that take on larger themes than you are currently working on.

3 Make three calls today to literary managers or producers telling them you are a writer (playwright, screenwriter, or TV writer) and that you have a new script, describing in one sentence what it is about. A newly appointed artistic director of a New York theater told me he read those projects first which agents or writers were able to explain clearly, succinctly, in one or two sentences, and with a sense of excitement.

Assignment

Track your plot. Is the action always moving the piece forward? If not, how can you keep it moving? Since character is action, what are your characters likely to do, given the escalating conflicts and obstacles? Double check there *are* escalating obstacles. Continue rewriting. Every rewrite affects the entire plot and may require revising other scenes.

Week 13
Lessons from master teachers and students

What they said

The primary definition of "education" in the Oxford English Dictionary is "a process of nourishment." I had always interpreted the word beginning with its Latin root, "to lead out." Both meanings are appropriate. Our work as educators is to lead in a nourishing, truthful manner, encouraging thoughtful writers who not only write horizontally (the plot) but vertically (depth). T. S. Eliot, in his essay *Tradition and the Individual Talent*, says that no artist has his complete meaning alone. Eliot goes on to say an entire order exists before the work. Therefore, the education of writers demands an awareness of all literature and history that precedes the moment the first line is put on the paper. Writers should read. One of the first questions I ask an incoming class is "What are you reading?" Ask the same of other writers and colleagues. The current global complexities demand thinking writers.

In thirty-five years of educating dramatic writers, I have tried to maintain principles of honesty, realistic encouragement, relentless rewriting, and an insistence on completion of projects. Occasionally there is the idea that fails to engage the writer's passion, and is therefore doomed to general failure. In those cases, the writer, with blessings, starts a new and more emotionally involved script. In cases where it is only a question of being stuck, we understand that is the writer's perpetual state. Our work is solving writing problems, finding the way out of the maze.

Talent is born, but the craft of writing has to do with the disciplined training and enlightenment of the artist. We, as teachers, often feel like a parent with a child; if only we could have them a little longer, we could help them become a better writer. What we hope is that each dramatist will feel the same about every script: *if only we could rewrite it one more time, it may come closer to perfection.*

What we *can* teach writers is to have honesty and the courage that their blue or red is a unique blueness or redness. They should have faith in the middle, when there is just the writer alone with a vision and no encouragement but their own iron will, empowered by a firm belief in the landscape they're burrowing through.

Freud said the two most important things in life are self-respect and pleasure. I urge my students to respect the instinct that stirred the work and to take pleasure in the journey.

There is not a writer who hasn't had a succession of mentors and teachers. As dramatic writers none of us exists in a vacuum. Who were yours? When I started tracing the ones who influenced and encouraged me, the list was long, and so I named it the "Army."

Here is my "Army," with its soldiers listed in chronological order, and what they taught me.

My mother, Dora, and her sister Helen were my first. They danced around the house where I grew up, on 703 Walk Hill Street in Mattapan, Massachusetts, clowning, and singing all the songs from the 1920s, 30s, and 40s. Their favorites were Eddie Cantor's *Josephina Please Don't Lean on the Bell,* Jimmy Durante's *Inka Dinka Doo,* and *Yes, We Have No Bananas,* sung by Al Jolson and later by Benny Goodman and Louis Prima. They knew every lyric. In our small kitchen, they'd perform, vaudeville style and in full costume, sometimes substituting, with delight, what they thought of as "off-color lyrics." My sister and I would roar with laughter. They were a regular Ziegfeld Follies.

Miss Evans, the sixth-grade teacher at the Martha Baker School in Mattapan, read from the Bible every morning. Her favorite was from Proverbs, "A good name is better than silver and gold." It's from her I first learned about story. The Bible remains a continuing resource.

Miss Sophia Palm was a teacher at Roxbury Memorial High School for Girls, in Roxbury, Massachusetts. My English teacher in our junior year, she had us write a short story every week. Ours was a commercial class, meant for women who were not planning on college. After the first weeks, she called me up and asked, "What are you doing in a Commercial Class? You are a writer." When I revealed my family could not afford college, Miss Palm drew up her small body defiantly. She signed me up for summer high-school college classes and guided me through the college application process, including viable scholarships. I was admitted to Radcliffe and Boston University, but it was Tufts that awarded a full tuition scholarship in 1953—six hundred dollars—so Tufts it was. And that made all the difference. Miss Palm and I exchanged Christmas cards for many years. The year no card arrived, I understood she was gone.

John Holmes, the poet, was a writing professor in freshman year at Tufts. John was a good friend of Robert Frost's, and when the poet came to campus to read *The Road Not Taken*, in his gravelly voice, it was this want-to-be writer who was chosen to introduce him at Goddard Hall. With gentle John at the helm, dozens of poems were written. (Later, a poem a week would be requested of my graduate dramatic-writing students. They were not critiqued, but rather offered as gifts at the beginning of every class.)

Many years then passed, spent in motherhood and wifehood, when Boston theater critic and playwriting teacher at Boston University, the eminent Elliot Norton, came into my life.

In 1967, the Women's Scholarship Association, a group who raised funds to send "needy Boston women" to college, wanted one of their "scholarship girls" to write a musical, commemorating their fiftieth anniversary. "You were a writer in high school and college, weren't you?" It was true: there were all those short stories for Miss Palm, and the poems for John Holmes. And so, *A Time To Remember,* about women in education was born: book, lyrics, and music. Sometimes, when you look back, there was a focus forming from the very beginning.

A long-dormant musical gene was awakened and I began to hear the music in my head. They presupposed that existing music from Broadway shows would be used, but my great-grandfather had been a musician and composer in Russia, and my father, a shoe salesman, served as the stand-by cantor for High Holidays. Also, it seemed I could play "by ear."

Elliot Norton, an invited guest, giving a talk on theater, was in the audience that day of the performance, and invited me to study with him at Boston University. "You're a playwright," he said. Maybe I was. What a thought!

In the next year, with Mr Norton as a dramaturg, my first drama was born. *Rousing Up the Rats Again* was about the holocaust and an imagined reunion of survivors and perpetrators. The script today is in a drawer, typed on yellow paper, the old-fashioned way, on my Smith-Corona. The paper has almost crumbled to dust. Mr Norton, known as the Dean of American Theatre Critics, remained a guide and support until he died in 2003. It was only luck that he was present that day to see *A Time to Remember.* It made all the difference.

The next mentor and lifelong friend was writer Barbara Greenberg, who continues as a mentor and teacher to the present day. Barbara was married to a surgeon on the staff of a Boston hospital, together with my first husband. Already an established writer when I met her, she proposed we write a children's musical together, based on her story *Jeremy and the Thinking Machine*. It was great fun writing that script. It was a true collaboration. (The children's musical had some local productions, and thirty years later, was produced by the National Theatre, London, and published by Samuel French, UK, in 2005.)

Shortly after *Jeremy* was finished, and I was about to accept a position teaching high-school English, I met with Barbara in her kitchen, over tea. Barbara asked what I would do in life if I could do anything. The answer took an instant. "Go to Yale and become a playwright, but that's ridiculous, with three children still in school in Boston." Barbara rose from the table, as quickly as I answered, went to the phone, and called Brandeis University. She returned announcing I had an interview with the chair of the theater department the following week. They only accepted three playwrights a year. And, oh yes, I was to send them a play. So, I applied with the only script I had, *Rousing Up the Rats Again*, and waited. They took me as one of three and I was on a dream path. It wouldn't have happened if Barbara hadn't asked that question that day.

Did I ever teach high school? As a substitute teacher at my children's junior high school, where, with my back turned to the class as I wrote on the chalkboard, the kids aimed paper airplanes at my head. Nothing personal. I *was* a substitute.

It was at Brandeis that playwright Israel Horovitz came into my life as a teacher and later friend. He had an old red Volkswagen bus, and I often joined him and his three kids, Adam (yes, of the Beastie Boys), Rachael, and Matthew (now producers), together with my three daughters. It was then the idea of being a playwright with a family first seemed possible. Israel taught me everything I know about playwriting—character, situation, humor, and tragedy, often quoting from his friend Ionesco. He was very proud of that friendship. More than that, in our second year, it was Israel who generously recommended my plays to the Goodman Theatre, even getting me an agent, his own Mary Dolan. It was from Israel I learned about being a generous teacher.

One note: when my new play *The Bridge at Belharbour* (written as a second-year grad student) was produced at Brandeis, the review was a good one, and was by then Boston Globe theater critic, Elliot Norton.

No one does it alone. Next came two remarkable women, playwright and poet Eve Merriam (*The Club*), and director Zelda Fichandler, who founded the Arena Stage Theatre in D.C., together with her husband Tom. It is Zelda who is credited with America's regional theater movement. I can't remember who came first, Eve or Zelda, but they knew each other and we three became what the boys nowadays call "buddies." It was Eve who told me never to write anything anyone else could easily write and it was Zelda who went on to produce three of my plays. The two were lifelong mentors.

Before moving to New York, while teaching at Harvard, I was introduced to the work of George Pierce Baker, the legendary educator at Harvard and Yale. While at Harvard he established Workshop 47 in the early 1900s (named after the course number), training some of the most notable American dramatists: Eugene O'Neill, Philip Barry, Sidney Howard, S.N. Behrman, and novelists John Dos Passos and Thomas Wolfe. He emphasized creative individuality and practical construction, guiding students' plays through workshop performances and fostering an imaginative realism.

In his book *Dramatic Technique* (1919), Baker writes, "Complete freedom of choice in subject and complete freedom of treatment are indispensable in the development of art." His papers and letters were recently released to the Harvard Theatre Collection, Houghton Library, which Professor Baker established.

In the spring of 1977, with productions at Manhattan Theatre Club (plays I had written while at Brandeis), Zelda Fichandler and I, both newly divorced, sublet a large studio overlooking West 12th Street. She would come in from Washington, D.C., I would come in from Boston, and Eve Merriam was always there, often with her friend set designer Robin Wagner. The two women writers attracted a stunning theatrical following, and so our apartment was filled with theater and literary luminaries. It was a hotbed, suffice it to say, and this young writer was wide-eyed and in heaven. Finally, here in New York, I was home. It was Zelda and Eve who kept me going creatively and spiritually. Those two made all the difference.

When I moved to New York permanently, working as a playwright and chairing the Dramatic Writing Department at NYU's Tisch School of the Arts, I would become mentor to thousands of writing students. It was fortunate I had good teachers.

At Tisch, my own mentors were the first two deans, David Oppenheim and then Mary Schmidt Campbell, now President of Spelman College. What were their best lessons? Honesty and grace under pressure. And then there were the students. They turn out to be our best teachers.

In our careers we stand on many shoulders. For me there have been writers: Richard Rhodes, Eve Merriam, Israel Horovitz, Mark Ravenhill, Tina Howe, Victor Lodato, and Barbara Greenberg, all of whom have taught me. Words are our business, but it's friendship that allows us to breathe.

The following dramatic writers were asked to share what they learned as students of writing and what they now teach.

Brandon Jacobs-Jenkin—US playwright; Dramatic Writing, New York University

Neighbors, Appropriate, The Octoroon, Gloria

What I learned

Sit through your own garbage and learn how to be in the "not-knowing." When I was a baby playwright, I would hate having to watch or hear things I'd written that I knew were bad because I would just be consumed with shame and humiliation and self-hatred and sometimes I would even go so far as run away from the reading, which, in retrospect, was insane. At some point, during some godawful reading of a play I've since abandoned, a fellow writer was like, "What are you doing? You have to sit through your own garbage. Otherwise you won't know how to clean it up." And it was true. Running away or hating myself was an extended form of perfectionism—and I wasn't going to be able to fix something unless I could experience how it was broken. It wasn't enough to know that something wasn't working. You had to hear it not work in order to diagnose it. And then you could fix it. And if you don't know how to fix it, you have to sit through it again. In the same way, you just sort of have to be where you are with the script. You have to wait with the mess until you know how to clean it up. I heard Lisa Kron once refer to this as "being in the not-knowing." You have to separate those feelings frustration/anger/shame associated with a bad draft or a "problem draft" from the simple fact that you just don't know. And then you can figure it out.

What I teach

One thing I'm always reminding my students is that we are in the art of illusion. We are creating an illusion of reality. Not reality itself. An audience is not there to see how accurately you depict what it's like to make a sandwich. We've all made sandwiches and, if we want, we can go to Subway and watch someone make sandwiches all day for free. Our job is to depict how making a sandwich can mean life, death, sadness, happiness, or whatever else. Similarly, I get a lot of students who assume that, because something happened to them and they thought it was interesting/they were moved, an audience is automatically going to find it interesting/be moved. No. No no no no no no no. Whether they are conscious of it or not, an audience is always asking itself the question: why should I care? Our first duty as storytellers is to answer that question.

Tina Howe—US playwright; Playwright-in-Residence, Hunter College, New York

Painting Churches, Coastal Disturbances, Pride's Crossing

What I learned

1 Playwriting is such an exhausting and ephemeral art form, it's essential to have some sort of family to come home to. A place where you can throw a fit, a pot, or a party. Plays close, but loved ones remain. To survive, you must have a life beyond the theater.
2 What do you do when a friend eagerly seeks you out after you've just seen their dreadful play? Lie. Always lie.
3 Never go to the theater without mints.

David Tolchinsky—US screenwriter, playwright, sound designer; Professor and Department Chair, Writing for the Screen and Stage, and Co-Director, Sound Design, Northwestern University

Sony Tri-Star's *Girl*, screenplay commissions from MGM, USA Networks, Disney, Ivan Reitman's Montecito Pictures, Edward R. Pressman Film Corp, Addis-Wechsler/Industry Entertainment, and the play *Clear*

What I learned

Most of this comes from Paul Luce, my teacher at USC (and these are all paraphrases based on my memories).

If your writing doesn't keep you up at night, it's not going to keep anyone else up at night.

When you're no longer telling your characters what to do and say and in fact they're refusing to do what you want them to do and instead they're doing things that are surprising and somewhat disturbing and you have the sense you're not making this up anymore but in fact your characters are ALIVE and now it's mainly your job just to keep up and write it all down before what they're doing and saying disappears, and more than this when you feel like your characters are AWAKE and LIVING even while you're sleeping, well then you're doing your job as a writer.

Someone will cut him/herself on a piece of paper. At first, there's no blood. You can barely see the cut. But if you wait long enough, the blood will appear.

What do you want the audience to come away with? To quote Maximus (as written by David Franzoni, John Logan, and William Nicholson) after he slaughters a bunch of guys in *Gladiator*: "Are you not entertained?" And after they've been entertained, I want audience members to talk about the film, to think about it, to dream about it, to let it burrow into their brains like some kind of hideous parasite. But if they're just engaged and not bored for 90 minutes, then great, I'm happy.

What I teach

Mostly story structure—four-act structure, mythic structure, sequence structure, scene structure, beginning, midpoint, dark moment, and ending. But the movies that affect me the most are the ones where the structures do not easily reveal themselves and are open-ended. *Mulholland Drive* comes to mind and so does *Ju On*. The film didn't really affect me while I was watching it, but it gave me nightmares because on the surface it didn't make any sense. My brain had to keep rolling it around. So maybe in some cases it's better to imply than to state.

Most writing doesn't happen at the computer. Most writing happens while you're taking a walk, a shower, watching a movie, or staring at a blank wall. When I first started living with my spouse Debra, she'd come home and I would be just staring into space... She said, "What are you doing?" I said, "Working..." And I was.

And I talk about the stories of Noah, Job, Jesus, and Moses as being models for many stories we tell. They also describe writing and writers. Noah was the first screenwriter in my mind. He had this crazy idea that it was going to rain and the earth was going to be destroyed and everyone mocked him until it actually rained. So he was proven right. But it's not a happy story for Noah. The world had to end for him to be proven right. The story of Noah is about the sacrifices we writers make, what we do to those around us, to complete our works, the isolation and depression we feel about being writers and the works we unleash on the world.

Be fearless. Be persistent. Be a nice person in real life, but be a total monster in your writing. Write monsters. Write monstrously. Write the scene you can't see in real life but it would be great to see. Write a dark wish. Write something that will change the world. Write something that you get up in the middle of the night to reread. And reread and reread.

Richard Walter—US screenwriter, novelist; Chair of Graduate Screenwriting, UCLA

The Essentials of Screenwriting, Escape from Film School (novel), *American Graffiti*

What I learned

Ideas are worthless. The creation of worthy dramatic narratives relies not upon ideas but stories.

What I teach

Recognize that a screenplay is at the most fundamental level nothing more than an elaborate list of sights and sounds. If you stick to sight and sound alone, and if every sight and every sound palpably, observably, identifiably moves the story forward, it doesn't matter what the script is about. It doesn't matter what is the so-called "genre." There are only two "genres": 1) good movies; 2) bad movies.

Barbara Greenberg—US poet, fiction writer, playwright; Goddard, Suffolk University, MIT

What I learned and what I teach

It was my mother who instilled in me, from babyhood on, a fascination with language. Long before I learned to read, she and I could recite by heart dozens of poems by Longfellow, Poe, and Wordsworth, as well as those of Mother Goose and Robert Lewis Stevenson. When, at age five, I too began to compose verses and playlets, she had me inscribe them in a dedicated notebook "like a real author."

None of this was formulaic, but it was certainly formative. My mother didn't live to see any of my adult writings published, nor could she have imagined me as a professor transposing her humble teachings for a college class. To read avidly. To respect the beauty and power of language. To engage in wordplay. To preserve one's ideas and phrases in notebooks and journals "like a real author."

Mark Ravenhill—UK playwright, essayist, TV writer

Shopping and Fucking, Mother Clap's Molly House, Some Explicit Polaroids, Totally Over You, Life of Galileo (translation), *A Life in Three Acts, Vicious* (for TV, with Gary Janeti), "By Any Means Necessary: Hamlet from Malcolm X to American Psycho"

What I teach

(From Mark Ravenhill's *Chekhov: Action!* workshop at the 2015 Venice Biennale, with permission of the author.)

The following is a summary of the exercises I devised for my workshop. We did these over five days, five hours a day.

1. Working the story muscle
   I read the Brothers Grimm tale "God Father Death" (chosen because it's not well known) aloud to the group. I stopped at three points during the reading and each time asked each person to write the next "beat" of narrative action themselves. The aim is not to guess what is in the Grimms' tale, not to be right or wrong. Nor to parody or "deconstruct." But to write what feels like the most pleasurable and most logical next beat of the story.
2. Family story
   What is the oldest family memory/story that is still told in your family? For example, there was a time in the war when your great-grandmother…. Write a monologue from the viewpoint of one of the participants in that event. Now write a second monologue from the perspective of another participant in that event (might be someone more marginal this time but still with a connection to the event).
3. Family mythology
   A discussion. Do families create an overall mythology about themselves. For example, we should be rich but the bastards stole everything or everyone in this family is a great character to whom hilarious things happen. Write a "headline" or several for your family's "myth."
4. Present action
   Take a section of *The Cherry Orchard* (a few pages) and rewrite it so that it consists entirely of dramatic action in the present. Cut

all "I remember" and "in the future" speeches and where you want to do so, replace them with present-tense events between the characters.

5 Substitute memories
Take the same section and replace all the "I remember" moments with lines/speeches using your own memories that parallel or resonate with the Chekhov characters. (This is rather like the way Lee Strasberg asked actors to use memory to work on a scene.) You may choose to have a dissonance in which Chekhov characters are speaking your memories or to rewrite the present-tense lines so that the whole scene becomes a contemporary scene.

6 Dramatic arc
Ask the whole group together to describe in a sentence the overall narrative action of *The Cherry Orchard*. A very simple story description—for example, "A family returns..." One of them writes it in big letters on a white board. It takes a long time but we found it absorbing and enjoyable. Then each person takes a page of the play, summarizes the dramatic action of that page, and tests the action of that page against our group description of the overall dramatic action.

7 Family rules
All families, I believe, have a set of often unspoken rules. Things like "Never do anything to make your father angry" or "Hard work is the most important thing not happiness." Write out the rules of your family (past or present or another family you know very well). Describe in some detail how each is enforced and by whom, what happens if you break a rule, etc. Swap the rules of your family with another writer. Each writer now writes a scene using this new set of family rules that they have been given. To give us a starting point for each scene, we chose simple situations from *The Cherry Orchard*— for example, "an elder sister helps her younger sister prepare for bed"—to give us the situations for the new scenes.

Kristoffer Diaz—US playwright, screenwriter, journalist; Dramatic Writing, Tisch School of the Arts, New York University, El Puente Academy for Peace and Justice

The Elaborate Entrance of Chad Deity (finalist for the 2009 Pulitzer), Welcome to Arroyo's (included in Daniel Banks's *Voices from the Hip-Hop Theatre*).

152 Lessons from master teachers and students

What I learned

FINISH. A completed script, even one full of holes and mistakes, is always an asset. It's a writing sample, a calling card, grist for development, and a cause for small personal celebration. An unfinished script, on the other hand, is *nothing*.

What I teach

(a) The world will not be changed by you not writing a play. No one else cares if you write a play. Rather than let that discourage you, take it as freedom. Write a play because you care desperately about writing it. Write a play because you need it. Never write plays for anyone else.

And (b) the world *may* be changed by you actually sitting down and writing a play. Rather than be intimidated by that, take it as an awesome challenge. Write a play that could change someone's life.

Femi Euba—*US playwright, director, actor, novelist;*
Professor of Black Drama, Louisiana State University

Archetypes, Imprecators and Victims of Fate: Origins and Developments of Satire in Black Drama, Poetics and the Creative Process: Organic Practicum to Playwriting, The Eye of Gabriel, Dionysus of the Holocaust, The Gulf.

What I learned

It was my playwriting professor at Yale (the late Richard Gilman) that first called my attention to the style I have come to adopt in my plays. In a playwriting workshop of my submission, a one-act, he began his critique-response by saying the play was "of course an extended metaphor." I churned that phrase "extended metaphor" over in my mind, seeing how it applied to that play and didn't think about it anymore after that. But then I found myself developing it more fully in my later full-lengths, such as *The Gulf* and *The Eye of Gabriel*. In both plays, the central idea is built on a word, a metaphor that develops with the plot to convey multiple meanings and perspectives of the word. For instance, in *The Gulf*, which explores the effects of Western mechanization on African traditional culture, the "gulf" of the title explores three levels of perception—the physical gulf, a scene of countless motor vehicle accidents; the gulf between pseudo-intellectuals and the ritual traditionalists; and, centrally, the gulf between the African and the African-American in the relationships each try to forge, albeit superficially. In *The Eye*, the five Gabriels of the play develop with the idea of the search for and passing of "black" power from the old generation to the new amid the conflicts of the central character. In fact, looking back at my earlier plays, I find that this stylistic inclination has been developing gradually in terms of my fascination for multiple meanings of words.

What I teach

I find myself constantly going back to the basics in the classroom—what I always refer to as "brass tacks," which is this: no matter whether a play is action- or idea-driven, there needs to be a central focus (through character or idea). It is this focus that informs the audience what that play is about, its objective, and how that objective is realized or not realized. For an audience needs to be engaged, and how better engage them from the outset than having a focused centrality with material conflicts, stakes, deadline, and commitment to the objective action or idea, or both.

Sabrina Dawhan—US screenwriter; Head of Screenwriting, Dramatic Writing, Tisch School of the Arts, New York University

Monsoon Wedding, Kaminey, Ishqiya; currently working on the stage version of *Monsoon Wedding*

What I learned

Protagonist drives the action. Seems pretty simple on the surface, but reminding myself of this has helped save many a script and scenes…

What I teach

Don't be afraid of the bad version. By this I mean, don't let the fear that it won't be any good paralyze you and get in the way of completing the work.

154   Lessons from master teachers and students

Steve Waters—*UK playwright, graduate of David Edgar's MA in Playwriting at University of Birmingham (a course which he later ran for several years); Senior Lecturer in Creative Writing, UEA, University of East Anglia*

Bretton Woods, Temple, Little Platoons, The Contingency Plan; The Secret Life of Plays; essays in *The Blackwell Companion to Modern British and Irish Drama* and *The Cambridge Companion to Harold Pinter*

What I learned

Way back in the 1990s I was a student of playwriting at the University of Birmingham under the great David Edgar; trying to summarize what I learned would be hubristic—perhaps the primary lesson as in all education was in observing the people around me, my peers and my teachers. They cared—about theater, about story, about the necessity of theater; the intensity of that care was instructive, the richness of memory and experience from which it emerged awesome. I learned I knew nothing and had to start again. I was laboring on a willfully obscure play, a play that deliberately shut out the audience that was resistant to discussion that imagined itself above the vulgarity of interpretation. David fearlessly revealed it to me as misguided, misconceived, and pretentious even; that this highly intelligent, politically motivated writer could be so indifferent to my work was of course a shock to my young vanity. I pleaded with him, "I just don't want to be obvious." He responded, with devastating wit, "I don't think that's going to be your problem."

What I teach

My constant refrain to writers is that they might become more themselves: to discover what it is they know uniquely and can tell uniquely. In a world of homogenization, the writer is one of the last refuges of the truly individuated voice. That's our only resource, and the last defense against big data and being replaced by drones. Finding their way of speaking right now in this age-old form seems to be all that is necessary; yet that's the hardest task of all.

James Felder—*US TV writer, comic-book editor, MFA graduate; Professor of Dramatic Writing, Tisch School of the Arts, New York University*

Teenage Mutant Ninja Turtles; well known for his work editing *Daredevil*

What I learned and what I teach

Some memories while I'm stirring gumbo in the kitchen... When I was a second-year grad in Dramatic Writing at NYU, I was taking a seminar in developing animated TV with Jon Collier (*The Simpsons, King of the Hill, Monk*). Someone in the class was pitching their project, and it went a little rough, but Jon started his feedback with, you're excited about it, and that's what counts—because if you don't care about it, you'll never make me care about it. I've had that communicated to me by so many teachers over the years, and always try to hammer it hard with students. I'm a bit of a structure junkie, but all the gears, and all the tricks only exist for one reason—to help the writer make the audience feel something deeply. Even if the story breaks all the rules and principles, if you can make the person out there laugh or cry, that's all that counts.

Tony Fisher—UK experimental screenwriter, filmmaker, philosopher; Senior Lecturer, Central School of Speech and Drama, UK

Film director: *The Trouble with Men and Women, Zdenka's Journey* (following one woman's journey through the nightmare of the Holocaust); "Heidegger and the Narrativity Debate" in *Continental Philosophy Review*

What I learned

Some years ago I was working with a script editor on a story that was proving extraordinarily difficult to get right. Reflecting on my difficulties, the editor remarked, "The problem is, Tony, you're trying to tell a complicated story using too complicated a structure. A complex story needs a simple structure, while a simple story needs to be told in a complex way." At the time that hit like a flash of lightening. Suddenly the whole thing made vivid sense, and the landscape of the story lit up with an extraordinary clarity. I've used that same advice with writers ever since, and it's seldom failed. There's a short "detective" story by Borges called "Death and the Compass," which also reflects on this dilemma of complexity/simplicity. The story culminates in an extraordinary exchange between the hapless detective Lönnrot and his nemesis Scharlach. But in that exchange, Lönnrot gives some great advice to writers, too, when he says to Scharlach: "In your labyrinth there are three lines too many." Now that is great advice, but what comes next is even better, when he says,

> I know of one Greek labyrinth which is a single straight line. Along that line so many philosophers have lost themselves that a mere detective might well do so If one succeeds in getting out of the Labyrinth, in finding one's home again, then one becomes a new being.

Well this is also great advice, and something I use frequently with students, for the way out of the labyrinth is indicated here— and it is this: like Odysseus at the start of the Odyssey, the hero is always "far from Ithaca," where he belongs. And his task is simply to get home; to get to Ithaca. Home/Ithaca might take many forms, but it is always bound to the answer to one fundamental question: what must the hero learn about himself or herself in order to attain their goal? Thus it is that heroes and writers enter the labyrinth in a state of ignorance, while the way out is always won at the cost of acquiring some knowledge of the self and its fallibilities.

Former students

Leah Franqui—playwright, winner of the Goldberg Prize and Sloan Foundation Prize

What I learned

The most important thing I was taught was how to be patient with myself. A lot of that comes down to process; and that's the larger thing I learned, how to appreciate my process of writing, how to be gentle with myself and hard on myself while crafting a play. There is a myth which I always believed that writers just sit down and write and it's perfect. I would write and I would think, why isn't my work perfect, why isn't it working? I didn't understand that it's a process, that a dramatic piece needs work and it also needs time to breathe. Some things work right off the bat and some don't, and it's realizing that some things will need more work, revisiting, trying, failing, and trying again, to function that really changed the way I thought about my writing. Knowing the stages of development, knowing how it evolves when I hear the lines out loud—that lesson has altered the way I write. Learning my process and letting myself work through it, each and every time, is the most valuable lesson I've learned, because it extends to every part of my writing: it spills over into character, finding them, letting their backstory bubble up in rich and interesting ways; plot, letting it come out of character desire; and structure, letting that be guided by them both. Knowing that it doesn't need to be perfect right out of the gate—that, in fact, it can't be—is freeing. It allows me to take chances, and to know that writing is a marathon, not a sprint. Patience can be taught—at least, with your writing.

Lauren Gunderson

2014 Steinberg/ATCA New Play Award for *I and You*; "One of the most produced playwrights in America in 2016" (*American Theatre Magazine*)

What I learned

How and when to cut. The answer to that being confidently and often. Not being precious about your own words leads to the flexibility and agility you need (especially given how collaborative playwriting ends up being in rehearsal) to make sure you tell the strongest, most compelling, least boring, most transformative story you can.

Benjamin Goldthorpe

The Lot, short film co-written with director Russell Blanchard

What I learned

Edward Albee once said very simply "Don't lie." Write honestly and find truth. That's been my mantra.

Robert B. Cohen, TV writer

Law and Order SVU

What I learned

The most important thing I learned was also the simplest: don't be boring. It is a cardinal sin. Even if you do everything else right, even if you have an important message, it is all for naught if you bore your audience. They are giving up their valuable, hard-earned time to listen to what you have to say—don't waste it. It's your duty as a writer to keep them engaged.

Week 14
To be a writer

Where we connect

There is a word in France describing the place where all the transportation centers connect: *correspondence*. We as writers are all connected, because our main work is to bond with the human condition, to show the face of it, its joys and battles.

Our stories are recorded from the drawings on prehistoric cave walls, through those told in the Bible, inscribed on the tombs of kings, the cemeteries of Prague, and the Mugao caves in China near the Gobi Desert, with its hundreds of Buddhas. Our writings are found in literature from London to Leningrad, Gaza to Jerusalem, Africa to China, to the cliff dwellings of Mesa Verde in Wyoming. It is all written.

We writers travel the road singly and together, in collaboration. It's sometimes bumpy and "under construction," because we are often lost when we are working, only to find out what we are writing about by the time we complete the first draft. Other times, it's a joy ride, and the script flows magically, like honey.

Some of you are at the beginning of your careers, some emerging, others in the middle. You can't foretell the entire topography until you've gone farther up the road. Only when you are nearing the end of your careers, can you see what you have accumulated and accomplished. In other words, it's never over until it is. For each of you it will be a different path. No one career resembles another. Look only to yourselves and for that genre and combination of work that's right for you. You'll recognize your own strength. It will be the place you excel.

Before a recent Kentucky Derby, a leading sportswriter speculated on what makes a good racehorse. He wrote:

> Horse races do not always go to the swift but are often won by the horse with the most endurance, the best ability to accelerate, to navigate traffic, unforeseen weather conditions—rain and mud,

running on a wet track. Romantics swear, also, by the importance of the will to succeed or what is called "heart." Then, given the best of everything, luck always plays a part.

This is true for writers also. The trick is to stay your course, write what you believe in, and be prepared for many rewrites. As Faulkner writes of one of his characters at the end of *The Sound and the Fury*: "She *endured.*" Be prepared to fight for your projects. Winning belongs to the long-distance runner. Stay in there. Stay in the race.

To be a writer brings responsibilities and joys. You are not promised a tranquil road, but nothing beats living the life you love, getting up every day and saying this is who I wanted to be and where I wanted to be, and with some minor adjustments, *I'm there.* One day you may find yourself sitting in a little cafe in Rome, there because of one of your projects, or doing research in Oxford, Beijing, or in the Hollywood Hills. You are there because you are a genuine working author, or even a "scribe." Phyllis Nagy, a playwright and screenwriter who has just won the New York Film Critics Circle Award for "Carol," was amused when one of the Los Angeles entertainment papers had a headline reading "'Carol' scribe pens new TriStar Film." Writer as scribe. Pretty nice.

For most of us, this is the realization of a dream, a dream some of us didn't even know we had when we were young.

What does it mean to be a writer? What is the price of our choice? The price, for one thing, is the certainty of some rejection and some failure. Understand that and let it never be a surprise to you. It's so for any profession that goes to the edge daily—doctors, dancers, pilots, zookeepers, mountain climbers, scientists, the butcher, the baker, the candlestick maker.

What then is the payoff for the writer? With certainty, you can count on your choice of subject unless working on a commissioned or outlined project. As a screenwriter or TV writer, although subject to other's editing, the process of how you get there always belongs to you. As a sitcom writer for TV, you will be using your innate sense of humor and people will be paying you to be funny and articulate. If you are writing for a dramatic series, you are following the story the producers have set out for you, but with selectivity and sharp dialogue. You are using, always, the innate talent you started with, together with the learned craft.

What else can we count on as writers? We can be assured of the act of creation. Architects have it, painters, weavers, composers, scientists, and designers—all making something where there was formerly thin air, where nothing existed.

Do writers have a moral responsibility? As storytellers and soul searchers, our collective morality has to be as questioners of our universe. This obligation also belongs to scientists and philosophers.

To be a writer is to head into the sun, to expand every day rather than retract. Our work has its origins with us, and therefore is original. The ideal work is audacious. It either fractures the heart or is in celebration of it. We have only to look to Taylor Mac's recent drama *Hir* for what Charles Isherwood, theater critic of the *New York Times*, calls the "dark vision of an American family run amok, the flawed and real humanity that simmers beneath the surreal comedy."

Our work is always to hold a light up to the cracks in people's lives, showing where the everyday bleeds at the heart.

To be a writer means, more than anything, we care about people and how they got to be the way they are. We understand what is "characteristic" of them, where it comes from and where it takes them. We recognize what they say—the spoken dialogue—and imagine what they're thinking or feeling. With our text and subtext we try to decipher veracity.

It is an honor and privilege to write for the theater, TV, and film and show audiences, their faces and their humanness. To be a writer means we have the freedom to fly, and that freedom is spectacularly precious.

You have the real possibility for success if you have the talent, the learned skills, the determination, and the belief in who you are as a writer. As author Eve Merriam told me, "Write what only you can write." Choose your own way to make that happen, whether you win a Pulitzer Prize or are cheered by the Academy, whether you write a children's book, like my former student Suzanne Collins, or a cookbook, like an earlier student, Adam Roberts. It all counts.

So go break a leg, break every record, break our hearts, and make us laugh, make us look truth in the eye and capture it with your words and images. Go with our hope, your hope, and all our blessings.

Graduation speech, Goldberg Department of Dramatic Writing, Tisch School of the Arts, New York University, May 2015

Congratulations

You have completed a first draft and one rewrite of your script.

Index

30 Rock 43

ABC (American Broadcasting Company) 9
Aeschylus 22
African American Review 98
African Queen, The 11, 34
After Marseilles 101–5
Agee, James 34
Agreement, The: comedy 119–22; humor 13–15; themes 7
Ahrens, Lynn 116
Albee, Edward xv, 109, 157
Alcott, Louisa May 1
Alda, Alan 113
All in the Timing 122
Almost in Vegas 8, 50
Altabe, Joan xii
ANC (African National Congress) 54
Angels in America 13
Apollinaire xiii
April in Paris 50
Aristotle xiii, 33
As You Like It 125
Astaire, Fred 2

Baker, George Pierce 25–6, 145
Balanchine, George 20
Bald Soprano, The 13, 123
Barrow Street Theatre 58
Barry, Philip 25, 145
Bartlett, Mike 117
Barton, Sue: series 1

beginnings (finding your story and telling it): characters 12–13; dramatic question 16; life experiences 9; locations 9–10; newspapers 10; play outline 13; screenplay outline 13–16; style 13, 15; *The African Queen* 11
Beijing Film Academy 17
Berlin, Irving 2
Berman, Monty 54–5
Berman, Myrtle 54–5
the Bible 94, 158
"Bible" (TV series) 18
"black" power 153
Black Sash (white women against Apartheid) 54
Blank, Jessica 113
Blazing Saddles 123–4
Blindspot 65
Blood Knot 5
Boesman and Lena 5
Bogart, Humphrey 34
Boraine, Alex 51, 116
"brass tacks" (central focus) 153
Brecht, Berthold 123
Bridge at Belharbor, The 7, 78–81, 86, 144
Bringing up Baby 118
Brooks, Mel 123
Brooks, Peter 67
Brown, Norman O. 131
Brownell, Julia 130
Brownowski, Jacob xiii, 104, 132
Buscemi, Steve 118

Campbell, Mary Schmidt 145
"Can Bad People Make Good Art"? xii
Cantor, Eddie 142
Carlson, Jeffrey 66
Carnelia, Craig 115
Carver, Raymond xv, 22, 32
Casablanca 64
Chaplin, Charlie 124, 126
Chayefsky, Paddy 6
checkpoints: common errors 91; dramatic projections (successful) 91–2; questions 90–1
Chekhov, Anton: flashlight moment xv; observation 10; people's lives xii, 74; rewriting 99; *The Cherry Orchard* 150–1; "The Lady with the Pet Dog" 10; *The Three Sisters* 73–5
Cherry Orchard, The 150–1
Chinatown 42
Churchill, Caryl 75
Clay, Jim 112
Clean House, The 61
Club, The 144
Cohen, Robert B. 132, 157
Collier, Jon 155
Collins, Suzanne 160
comedy: authors 125–30; farce 123; introduction 118–19; Manhattan Punchline Theater 122; parody 123–4; physical comedy 124; satire 123; *The Agreement* 119–22; when comedy works 128–9
comedy authors: Brownell, Julia 130; Craig, Ryan 127–8; Howe Tina 126; Ives, David 126; Johnson, Judith 128; Joseph, Rajiv 129–30; Kaplan, Steve 128–9; Lumet, Jenny 126; Nagy, Phyllis 127; Ravenhill, Mark 125–6; Stenham, Polly 127; Udko, Zack 130
Coming Home 64–5, 86
commedia del'arte (slapstick comedy) 124

complex characters: biographical questions 19–20; complexity 20–1; observation 22; plot 22; questions 18–19; reading 22; what the character does 21; what the character says 21; what others say about the character 21
"complex" definition 93–4
complexity/simplicity 155–6
conflict definition 32
conflicts escalation: change 34–5; confrontation 35; description 32–6
Copley Square Library, Boston US 134
correspondence 158
"Country Doctor, A" 127
Country of My Skull 51
Country Unmasked, A 51, 116
Cover Girl 2
Craig, Ryan 127–8
Culkin, Macauley 118
Culture Project, The 58
Curse of the Starving Class 76–7

Davidson, Gordon 113
Dawhan, Sabrina 153
de Caprio, Leonardo 114
"Death and the Compass" (short story) 155
Death of a Salesman 118
DeMott, Robert 110
dialogue: action 26; characterization and motivation 26; clichéd 24; "do not overwrite" 24; excessive "talk" 25; exterior 26; interior 26; motivation 23; selection 24–5
Diaz, Junot 22
Diaz, Kristoffer 151–2
Dickens, Charles 22
Dickinson, Emily 2
Didion, Joan xi, 5, 132
Dillon, John 35
Divorce Italian Style 119
Doctorow, E. L. 16
Dolan, Mary 4, 144

Index   163

Dr Strangelove 123
Dramatic Technique 26, 145
Dramatist Guild of America 107, 131
Dramatist Guild (journal) 116
Dream Deferred 69–70
Drew, Nancy: mystery series 1
Durante, Jimmy 141

Edgar, David 154
Ehn, Eric 135
Eliot, T. S. 141
endings: *A Raisin in the Sun* 69–71, 77; *After Marseilles* 81–8; *Blindspot* 65; *Casablanca* 64; *Curse of the Starving Classes* 76–7; definition 64; *Far Away* 75–6; *Gone with the Wind* 64; *Last Easter* 66; *Orange is the New Black* 65–6; *Shining City* 68–70; *The Bridge at Belharbour* 78–81, 86; *The Sisters Rosenweig* 71–3; *The Three Sisters* 73–5, 77
English Club 1–2
Environmental Film Festival, Washington D.C. xii
"Essay on Comedy" 124–5
Euba, Femi 152–3
Euripides xv, 22
Evans, Miss (teacher) 142
Everybody Loves Raymond 45
Exhibition 7, 41
Exonerated, The 58, 113
Eye Gabriel, The 152–3

fact, fiction and further: *A Question of Country* 115–7; fact 107–8, 114; novels 109; "Postulation" 117; *QED* 113; *The Grapes of Wrath* 109–12
"Family in Modern Drama, The" 67
Far Away 75–6
Farewell to Arms, A 96–7
Felder, James 154–5
Feydeau, Georges 123
Feynman, Richard 113

Fichandler, Zelda 12, 55, 58, 144–5
Fisher, Tony 155–6
Flea in Her Ear, A 123
Fonda, Henry 109
Ford, John 109
Ford, Richard 5
Forester, C. S. 11, 34
Forty-Eight Hours 33
Four Weddings and a Funeral 118
Frankl, Victor 104
Franqui, Leah 156–7
Frasier 46
Freud, Sigmund 129, 131
Friends 125
Frost, Robert 2, 143
Frost/Nixon 12
Fugard, Athol 5–6, 57

Gabler, Hedda 81
Galati, Frank 109–12
George, Madeleine 135
Gilbert and Sullivan 2, 123
Gilman, Richard 152
Gladiator 148
Glass Menagerie, The xv
Glee 45
Gloria Safer Agency 4
Gluck, Louise 5
Goetz, Ruth and August 109
Goldthorpe, Benjamin 157
Gone with the Wind 64
Good Will Hunting 42
Goodman, Benny 141
Grace and Frankie 34
Grapes of Wrath, The 109–12
Greenberg, Barbara 5, 97, 143–5, 149–50
Guardian 10
Guare, John 66
Gulf, The 152–3
Gunderson, Lauren 157

Haas, Robert 5
Hall, Donald 5
Hamlet 123

Hammett, Dashiel 134
Handke, Peter xi
Hansberry, Lorraine 69, 71, 77
Harburg, Yip 50
Harvard Theatre Collection, Houghton Library 26, 145
Havel, Vaclav xi
Hayner, Patricia 116
Hayworth, Rita 2
Heard, Elisabeth J. 98–9
Heiress, The 109
Hellman, Lillian 134
Hello and Goodbye 5
Hemingway, Ernest 96, 97
Hepburn, Katherine 34
High Noon 34
Hir 123, 160
Hog Alley 6, 9
Holmes, John (Tufts University) 1, 143
Holy Rosenbergs, The 128
Home Alone 118
Horovitz, Israel: agent 4; clarity 96; dramatic question 16; last word 64; teacher/friend 144; write outside the box 41; writers 145
Hot in Cleveland 45
Houghton, Jim 60
House of Cards 44, 132
Howard, Sidney 25
Howe, Tina 100–1, 126, 145, 147
Hughes, Langston 69
humor: serious subjects 119; *The Agreement* 13–15
Hunter, Lew 33
Huston, John 34

I Love Lucy 44
Identity of Man, The xiii, 104, 132
Inka Dinka Doo 141
Ionesco 13, 123
Irving, John 5, 109
Isherwood, Charles (critic) 160
Ives, David 122, 126

Jacobs-Jenkin, Brandon 146–7
James, Henry 109

Janneti, Gary 119
Jenkin, Len 127
Jensen, Erik 113
Jeremy and the Thinking Machine 97, 144
JFK (film) 11
Jim Gaffigan Show, The 46
Jitney 97–8
Johnson, Judith 128
Johnson, Nunally 109
Jolson, Al 141
Joseph, Rajiv 129–30
Ju On 148

Kafka, Franz 127
Kaplan, Steve 122, 128–9
Keaton, Buster 126
Keats, John xiv
Khan, Ricardo 60
King Charles III 117
Krog, Antjie 51
Kron, Lisa 146
Kubrick, Stanley 123
Kushner, Tony 13, 25

La Jolla Playhouse 109
"Lady with the Pet Dog, The" 10
Labantu, Ikamva 51, 58
Lange, Jessica 134
Last Easter 66
Lavery, Bryony 66
Law and Order SVU 132
Layton, Robert 113
Lee, Leslie 60
lessons from master teachers and students: Campbell, Mary Schmidt 145; Dora Danis (mother) 142; dramatic writers 146–56; Evans, Miss 142; Fichandler, Zelda 144–5; former students 156–7; Greenberg, Barbara 143–5; Helen (sister) 142; Horovitz, Israel 144–5; introduction 141–6; Merriam, Eve 144–5; Norton, Eliot 143–4; Opppenheim, David 145; Palm, Sophia 142

lessons from master teachers and students – dramatic writers: Dawhan, Sabrina 153; Diaz, Kristoffer 151–2; Euba, Femi 152–3; Felder, James 154–5; Fisher, Tony 155–6; Greenberg, Barbara 149–50; Howe, Tina 147–8, 147–9; Jacobs-Jenkin, Brandon 146–7; Ravenhill, Mark 150–1; Walter, Richard 149; Waters, Steve 154
lessons from master teachers and students – former students: Cohen, Robert B. 157; Franqui, Leah 156–7; Goldthorpe, Benjamin 157; Gunderson, Lauren 157
Letters upon the Aesthetic Education of Man xiv
Levine, Philip 5
Little Women 1–2
Living in Truth xi
Lodato, Victor 145
Lolita 109
"Long Ago and Far Away" (song) 2
Look Ma We're Dancing 8
Luce, Paul 147
Lumet, Jenny 126

Mac, Taylor 123, 160
McCarter Theatre 57
McCarthyism xii
McCauley, Robbie 59
McPherson, Conor 68
Makeba, Miriam 54
Malamud, Bernard 93
Mamet, David 23
Mandela, Nelson 54, 115–16
Manhattan Punchline Theater (MPT) 122
Mankiewicz, Herman 139
Mann, Emily 57
Man's Search for Meaning (Victor Frankl) 104
Marx Brothers 124, 126
Masekela, Hugh 54–5
Mattaplan Free Library, Boston US 1

Maxwell, William xv
Meredith, George 124
Merriam, Eve 134, 144–5, 160
Midnight Cowboy 42
Miller, Arthur: *Death of a Salesman* 118; missing happiness 32; moral dilemma xiv; "The Family in Modern Drama" 67; tragedy xvi, 118; "Tragedy and the Common Man" 12
Milton, John 16
Milwaukee Rep 35
Molière 125–6
moral responsibility: artists xi–xxii; writers 160
Morgan, Peter 12
Morrison, Toni 22
"mosaic" school of thought 33
Mother Courage 123
Mulholland Drive 148
My Brilliant Career 41

Nabakov, Vladamir 109
Nagy, Phyllis 127, 159
National Theatre, London 109, 128, 144
NCIS New Orleans 44–5
Negro Ensemble Company (NEC) 60
Network (film) 6, 9
New Criticism school xi
New York Magazine 122
New York Theatre Workshop 76
New York Times 10, 83, 160
Nicola, James, C. 76
'Night, Mother 96
Noises Off 123
Norman, Marsha 96
North by NorthWest 41
Norton, Elliot (theatre critic) 3, 143–4
notebooks 7–8, 20
Notebooks of Athol Fugard, 1960–1977 5–6
Nurse Jackie 129–30

Index

"Ode on a Grecian Urn" xiv
Odyssey, the 156
Office, The 45
Oklahoma 2
On the Town 40
O'Neill, Eugene xiv, 25, 118, 145
Opppenheim, David 145
Orange is the New Black 65–6
Orton, Joe 118
Our Town xv
Out of Order 7
Over the Rainbow 50
Owens, Louis 110

Palm, Sophia (teacher) 142
Paradise Lost 16–17
Parnell, Peter 109, 113
Piano Lesson, The 61
Plague, The 3
Platt, Oliver 122
Playwrights at Work 78
Playwrights in Rehearsal 78
Plaza Suite xv
Poetics 33
Poore, Charles 97
Poster Boy 116
Pound, Ezra xii
Prima, Louis 141
Prindle Institute for Ethics, DePauw University xxii
Pulp Fiction 42
putting it all together – *A Question of Country* 49–62

QED 113
Question of Country, A: dialogue 26–9; fact, fiction and further 115; production 49–62; script xvii–xxi; themes 7–8
questions (sixty) to ask when writing dramatic pieces 38–47

Radiohead (band) 127
Ragtime 116
Raisin in the Sun, A 69–71, 77
Ravenhill, Mark 119, 125–6, 145, 150–1
Readings for the Plot 67
rewriting 93–101

Rhodes, Richard 5, 145
Road Not Taken, The 2, 143
Roberts, Adam 160
Rockefeller Grant (Bellagio) 55
Rogers, Ginger 2
Room of One's Own, A 134–5
Rousing Up the Rats Again 3, 7, 143–4
Rubin, Barbara 57
Ruhl, Sarah 61

St Augustine xi
Scarred Lands, Wounded Lives xi
Schiller, Friedrich xiv
Schlesinger Library, Radcliffe University 3
Science and Human Values xiii
Scott, George C. xv
Screenwriting 33
Scribner's Magazine 97
Seinfeld 45
Sevuch, Ralph 107
Shakespeare, William 12, 117
Shanghai Normal University, Xian 36
Shepard, Sam 76, 134
Shining City 68–70
Silkwood 9
Simon, Neil xv
Sisters Rosenweig, The 71–3
Skin of Our Teeth, The 123
Sleeping Beauty 66
Slouching Towards Bethlehem xi
Small Delegation, A xvi–xvii, xxi, 7, 32–3, 50
Smith, Niegel 61
So Long, See You Tomorrow xv
Social Network, The 12
Sondheim, Stephen 13
Sophocles xi, 138
Sorkin, Aaron 12
Sound and the Fury, The 159
Southernmost, Tip, The 8
Special Victims Unit 45
Stapleton, Maureen xv
Statues 7
Steinbeck, John 109
Stenham, Polly 127

Stone, Oliver 12
Streep, Meryl 21
Sypher, Wylie 124–5

Taylor, Myra 57–8
Thelma and Louise 12
Three Sisters, The 73–5
Three Stooges 124
Time to Remember, A (show) 3, 143
Tisch School of the Arts 6, 8, 88, 117, 145, 160
Titanic 114
Tolchinsky, David 147–9
Tolstoy 22
Tommy, Liesel 57
Tradition and the Individual Talent 141
"Tragedy and the Common Man" 12
Traze, Joe 115
Truth in Comedy 130
Truth and Reconciliation Commission, South Africa 54, 115
Tusk Tusk 127

Udko, Zack 130
Ungodly, The 5
Unspeakable Truths 116

Veh, Molly 6–7
Venus in Fur 123
Vicious 118–19
Vietnam War 6
Voigt, Ellen Bryant 4–5

Wagner, Robert 145
Walter, Richard 4, 149
Washburne, Anne 135
Washington Square 109
Wasserstein, Wendy 71
Watergate 6
Waters, Steve 154
Wet Hot American Summer: First Day of Camp 45
When Harry Met Sally 42
White, E. B. 129
Whites Who Fought Apartheid, The (radio documentary) 55
Who's Afraid of Virginia Woolf? xv
Wilder, Thornton xv, 123
Wille, Donald 6, 114
Williams, Tennessee xiv
Wilson, August 60, 97–9
Witness 33
Wizard of Oz 50
Wolf, Greg 5
Wolf, Tobias 5
Wolfe, Thomas 25, 145
Women's Scholarship Association (WSA) 1–2, 143
Woolf, Virginia 1, 134–5
Writer's Army 135

Year of Magical Thinking, The (Joan Didion) 5
Yimou, Zhang 64
Yorke, Thom 127

Ziegfeld Follies 142

Taylor & Francis eBooks

Helping you to choose the right eBooks for your Library

Add Routledge titles to your library's digital collection today. Taylor and Francis ebooks contains over 50,000 titles in the Humanities, Social Sciences, Behavioural Sciences, Built Environment and Law.

Choose from a range of subject packages or create your own!

Benefits for you
- Free MARC records
- COUNTER-compliant usage statistics
- Flexible purchase and pricing options
- All titles DRM-free.

Benefits for your user
- Off-site, anytime access via Athens or referring URL
- Print or copy pages or chapters
- Full content search
- Bookmark, highlight and annotate text
- Access to thousands of pages of quality research at the click of a button.

REQUEST YOUR **FREE INSTITUTIONAL TRIAL TODAY**

Free Trials Available
We offer free trials to qualifying academic, corporate and government customers.

eCollections – Choose from over 30 subject eCollections, including:

Archaeology	Language Learning
Architecture	Law
Asian Studies	Literature
Business & Management	Media & Communication
Classical Studies	Middle East Studies
Construction	Music
Creative & Media Arts	Philosophy
Criminology & Criminal Justice	Planning
Economics	Politics
Education	Psychology & Mental Health
Energy	Religion
Engineering	Security
English Language & Linguistics	Social Work
Environment & Sustainability	Sociology
Geography	Sport
Health Studies	Theatre & Performance
History	Tourism, Hospitality & Events

For more information, pricing enquiries or to order a free trial, please contact your local sales team:
www.tandfebooks.com/page/sales

 The home of Routledge books

www.tandfebooks.com